GLENN MAXWELL

AUSTRALIAN CRICKETER

MR VIVEK KUMAR PANDEY SHAMBHUNATH

Short biography of Glenn Maxwell and about life .During writing this book no character & no religious are harmed written by Mr Vivek Kumar Pandey. winner youngest writer award 1st rank in india 2020.He is only one writer can publish 700+ own book that was greatest successfull in his life. This All Credit Goes To My Super Hero Daddy.

Contents

Foreword

Author biography in English :MY NAME IS VIVEK KUMAR PANDEY . I WAS BORN IN 30 SEP 2002,I AM FROM SURAT GUJARAT INDIA.MY DREAM WAS TO BE GOOD WRITERS ,MY FAMILY SUPPORTED ME TO SUCCESSFUL AND I CAN DO IT MY SELF.How do I write? That is a question, I believe, that can be honestly answered by me."CELEBRATING YOUNGEST WRITER AWARD WINNER IN GUJARAT 1ST RANK" MR PANDEY JI . I may think I did a good job writing something when in reality it could be horrible. The reader is the one who decides the quality of my writing. I do find writing to be natural to me and therefore find it to be a real challenge. My trick as a challenged writer is to do the best I can and know that I am happy with the final outcome. It may take a while to do my best and there may be quite a few problems I run into along the way.

I am not a greedy person those who are thinking about me and my self I never tried it anyone people suffering from sadness ,I trying to get promoted people suffering from happiness and joy in your Life Time. Now in current situation in India and also world people are unemployed and have no many but our indian governor help to people to get free food from ration card , i also take part in leadership team ,i am Motivational speaker , Film script writer. There was my two dream firstly writer and secondly actor & also my own film is upcoming soon i done almost completely completed script for my film .I AM GOING TO SAY WORD OF HEART TOUCH OUT PLEASE READ IT" , firstly i thanks my father he supports me in this field they always getting inspired me by own his words and behavior ,they always said that he was a biggest person in the world in future and also they purchase fruit and chocolate for me in anytime & anyway , firstly my father buy him then call me Vivek you want a chocolate i will say yes papa but how many tell me ,papa: you tell me how much i buy him i told 1 or 2 chocolate but my father purchase whole the boxes of chocolate and they get suprised me. MY FATHER WAS BORN IN " 20 SEPTEMBER" 1971 IN INDIA.

1) MY FATHER FAVORITE CLOTHES IS KURTA PAIJMA AND ALSO STYLES SHOE

2) FAVORITE SINGER IS KISHORE DA

3) FAVORITE STATE GUJARAT AND KOLKATA , HIS VILLAGE IN BIHAR

4) FAVORITE COLOR BLACK AND WHITE

THEY ALSO LOVE cricket like IPL and one day t-20 .they also like watching a News daily and heard the song daily ,they also interested in tik tok video but in current time tik tok is banned in india but also few videos are in you tube. In lockdown time my family and me very enjoy day daily. my father play daily ludo with his sister and son, daughter.they always loved tea and coffee anytime call me "। विवेक थोडा़ चाय बनाओना विवेक तुम्हारे हाथ का चाय अच्छा लगता है". I make it tea for my father but some reason after the April to june they are suffering from fever and cough , weakness on 6 June 2020 my father death. they not told me say bye bye his life. After death of 6 June on 10 june my mom and dad anniversary.but my father is Best in the world they can do anything for me please take care of father and respect it of your parents.

CHAPTER ONE

Glenn Maxwell

- Glenn Maxwell

1. During writing this book no character & no religious are harmed written by Mr Vivek Kumar Pandey.

Glenn James Maxwell (born 14 October 1988) is an Australian professional international cricketer, who currently plays ODI and Twenty20 cricket for Australia. He has also played Test cricket for Australia. He represents Victoria and Melbourne Stars in Australian domestic cricket.

He began his professional cricketing career playing for Victoria in the Twenty20 Big Bash in 2010.He is known for his dramatic shot making and improvisation in the short form of the game, scoring 102 from 52 balls against Sri Lanka in the 2015 World Cup, the second fastest World Cup century to date. He also scored an unbeaten 145* from 65 balls against Sri Lanka in 2016, the fourth highest score in Twenty20 Internationals.

Despite his power hitting in the short form of the game, he has shown ability in the longer form of the game including a maiden Test century against India in Ranchi on 16 March 2017 in which he scored 104 from 185 balls. In doing so he became the second Australian to score centuries in all three formats after Shane Watson, joining an elite club of only 13 other cricketers that have achieved this feat. On 24 November 2017 he scored his maiden double century in the Sheffield Shield competition. He was dismissed for 278 from 318 balls in an innings which included 36 fours and four sixes.

In 2011, he set the record for the fastest ever half-century in Australian domestic one day cricket, scoring 50 runs off 19 balls. In February 2013, the Indian Premier League team the Mumbai Indians bought him for $1 million

US. In March 2013, he made his Test debut against India in the second Test at Hyderabad.

On 28 March 2018, Maxwell was urgently recalled to the Test squad, along with Matthew Renshaw and Joe Burns, following the suspensions of Steve Smith, David Warner and Cameron Bancroft for ball tampering during the Third Test of the Australian 2018 Tour of South Africa. In October 2019, he announced an indefinite break from the game to deal with mental health difficulties.

- Early life

Maxwell was born in Kew, Victoria, and played his junior cricket for South Belgrave CC. He began his cricket as a pace bowler, before remodelling his run-up and becoming an off spin bowler. Despite that, he also has a deceptively powerful and accurate throw to effect run-outs.Maxwell's teammates and the media gave him the nickname "The Big Show" due to his confidence and his tendency to play extravagant shots, especially a wide array and variations of sweep shots. He however prefers the nickname "Maxi".

Glenn Maxwell during a BBL match while playing for Melbourne Stars

- domestic career

Maxwell joined the Victorian squad in July 2009. He was called into the FDR squad in November when Andrew McDonald was injured. Maxwell played in the 2010 Hong Kong Cricket Sixes tournament and was named Player of the Tournament as Australia became champions for the first time.

Maxwell was selected to play for the Australian Institute of Sports in the 2010 Emerging Players Tournament. He scored 63 against India in the semi-final.

Maxwell made his first-class debut for Victoria against NSW in 2010–11. He took two catches, two wickets and scored 38. He leapt to national attention when he scored a match winning 51 off 19 balls in a Ryobi Cup game against Tasmania. It was the fastest half century in Australian domestic one day history.

- He followed this with an excellent Shield game against South Australia, scoring 63 and 103, and taking three catches, winning the Man of the

Match Award. He scored 38 (the top score of the innings) and 61 against Queensland.In the 2011 Emerging Players Tournament, Maxwell scored 59 off 23 balls in a game against India. He then made 110 off 52 balls against South Africa in a losing cause.

Maxwell began the 2011–12 season well against Queensland, making 4 and 32 and taking three wickets. He followed this with 92 against New South Wales. Maxwell took 2/30 and 3/36 against Tasmania, but only scored 2 and 10 with the bat. He made 61 and 72 against Western Australia and took two wickets. In the second Victoria-WA game he scored 43 and 0 and took two wickets. Maxwell made 26 and 43 against New South Wales.

- He scored 65 and took 2 wickets against Queensland. In a Ryobi Cup game against Queensland, Maxwell scored 50 off 37 balls. In the BBL Maxwell scored 124 in six innings for the Melbourne Renegades. He was briefly injured in January.

Maxwell went to England to play club cricket for South Wilts and Hampshire Second XI. He played T20 for Hampshire. He played for Hampshire Second XI against Essex, scoring 66 and taking 1 for 12 in six overs. He then played T20: 32 from 12 balls against Sussex and 115 from 31 balls against MCC Young Cricketers. He scored 178 runs at 59.33 and a strike rate of 178 for Hampshire in the county Twenty20 competition.Maxwell batting for Lancashire during a Royal London One-Day Cup match in 2019.

Maxwell began the 2012–13 summer well, scoring 58 off 53 balls in a Ryobi Cup game. He scored 51 in a Shield game against Tasmania. Against New South Wales, Maxwell took 2/12 and 0/50 and made 39 with the bat. In a Shield game against South Australia, Maxwell scored a pair, but took 4/42 with the ball, his best bowling effort at first-class level to date.

Maxwell attempted to transfer to the NSW team for the 2016–17 summer but was refused. Maxwell was dropped from the Victorian side for the first match of the 2016–17 Sheffield Shield season. "He should have been playing," said test selector Mark Waugh. "From an Australian point of view, he's quite capable of playing Test match cricket. You need to be asking the Victorian selectors why they left him out. It surely can't be cricket-related because he would be in the team."Maxwell was picked in the next Shield game and scored 81. He scored 10and 3 against NSW, 6 and 29 against South Australia.

In the first Shield game of the 2017-18 year, Maxwell made 7 and 20. He scored 60 and 64 in the next game, against South Australia. In the third round, playing for Victoria against Tasmania, Maxwell scored 4 and 45 not out; in the second innings he played for 115 balls and helped Victoria draw the rain-shortened game.

- International career

Maxwell was picked for the UAE tour of 2012. Head selector John Inverarity said Maxwell was "a versatile and lively off-spinning allrounder and brilliant fieldsman... Glenn will provide another spin bowler option on the slow, low, turning wickets in the UAE."

Maxwell made his ODI debut for Australia against Afghanistan in a one-off One Day International in the United Arab Emirates in 2012. He scored 2 and took 0-21. In his 2nd ODI, playing against Pakistan, he hit 38 off 38 balls, helping rescue Australia from a tricky 5–121 to victory. He followed it with 28 off 27 balls and 0-37 off 4 overs in the second ODI, but in a losing course. In the third ODI he scored an unbeaten 56, including a six to seal victory for Australia; he also took 0-33.

Maxwell then played in two T20I games against Pakistan in the same tour. In his debut he scored 4 and opened the bowling, taking 0-25. In third T20I, he made 27 off 20 balls and took 1-12.

- 2012 ICC World T20 Cup

Maxwell was picked in Australia's squad to play in the 2012 ICC World Twenty20 in Sri Lanka. During press conference he said that, "I'm very confident I can perform now at this level. "Hopefully I can be that x-factor that Australia needs to win this tournament... That could mean a run out, a brilliant catch, a breakthrough wicket with the ball or big hitting. I'm really embracing that 'x-factor' tag. I don't really have too many doubts, I don't think I'm going to try to back down any time soon either."

He did not have a memorable tournament though, with returns of 1–12 against Ireland 0–17 against the West Indies, 0-11 and 4 against India, 0–7 against South Africa, and 0-6 and 4 against Pakistan.Australia reached semi-final of the tournament, where they lost the match to West Indies.

- 2012–13

Maxwell was picked in the Australian A side to play South Africa, replacing an injured Jon Holland. Selector John Inverarity said when he spoke to Maxwell he "said 'you're the spinner, you're in the hot seat, get on with it', and we hope he responds to that sort of challenge. Glenn is a player of particular interest, a player of great skill and exuberance and enthusiasm. We want him as an allrounder, so we're very keen for him to get opportunity with his spin bowling, and we're putting him in the hot seat here." Maxwell scored 64 and took 2/70.

Maxwell was picked for the Cricket Australia Chairman's XI against Sri Lanka, scoring 91 off 77 balls and taking 1/127 with the ball.

Maxwell was brought into the Australian squad for the third test against Sri Lanka to replace Shane Watson. ""Glenn brings that allrounder package," said skipper Michael Clarke. "He's scored plenty of runs for Victoria with the bat, I think he averages over 40 with the bat in first-class cricket, and he's had success with the ball. He's the full package and he has that X-factor about him." Maxwell did some work with Shane Warne to help with his bowling.

- 2012-13 ODI Series

On 10 January 2013, he played his first ODI at home against Sri Lanka, being involved in two run outs off consecutive balls. He made 5 and 0-28. In other games against Sri Lankans he made 8 and 0-19,9 and 0–6.The series drawn 2-2.

He was involved in a controversy in the 2nd T20 against Sri Lanka when involved in a verbal altercation against Sri Lankan players after failing to hit the last ball for four.

On 1 February 2013, he scored 51* (from 35 balls) as an opener as Australia chased down the target of 71 set by the West Indies in their first ODI of the series.On 3 February in the series' 2nd ODI in Perth, he scored a duck, but took 4/63 with the ball to support Mitchell Starc (5/32) and help bowl out the visitors for 212 in 38.1 overs. In the last two games he took 4 and 1-44, and 1-34 and 1.

- 2013: Test debut year

Maxwell was picked on the 2013 2012-13 Indian tour. Australia was hoping to use him as an all rounder despite erratic bowling form.

"Maxwell has bowled extremely well, he is getting better and better," said coach Mickey Arthur. "One of the things we've sat down and said is if you want to be the spinning all-rounder you've got to put a huge amount of time into your bowling, because Maxy would always try to bowl the miracle ball and then he'd bowl a leggie, then try a doosra, he just didn't settle on anything. All we've got him in the nets is bowling offspin, offspin, offspin. It's repetition all the time and he's getting better and better at it. He's a very fast learner."

"I feel like I'm definitely a genuine batsman," Maxwell said. "I've done a lot of work on my technique over the last few years... I've played some good Shield innings where I've played technically really good cricket... I'm sure if I get the chance to play Test cricket I'll probably be a bit more reserved."

In March 2013, he made his Test debut against India in the second Test at Hyderabad. He was included as the second spinner in the team, supporting Xavier Doherty (Nathan Lyon had been dropped and Steve O'Keefe was not taken on the tour). Maxwell failed to impress with the bat, making 13 and 8 in the first and second innings respectively, but took 4/127 with the ball.

He was dropped from the team in the third Test as Australia went with more specialist bowlers. He made a comeback in the fourth and final Test in Delhi due to a Michael Clarke injury. However he failed again with the bat making just 10 and 8.

In June 2013, during 2013 ICC Champions Trophy Maxwell scored 29 off 22 balls against New Zealand. Against Sri Lanka, he scored 32 off 20 balls in a losing course. Australia knocked out from tournament in early stages.

Maxwell missed selection for the 2013 Ashes but was picked to play for Australia A in a tour of South Africa. He scored 61 and 25 against Zimbabwe A, and 155 and 17 against South Africa A (taking 1/78) then making a pair and taking no wickets in a second game against South Africa A. In the one day tournament, he scored 145 off 79 balls, and 93 against India A.

Maxwell returned to India in October as part of an Australian limited over team tour of India. Maxwell made 31 off 23 balls, 53 from 32 balls and 0-48, 1-8 and 3, 92 off 77 balls, 9 and 0/40, and 0-32 and 60 off 22 balls. India won the 7-match series 3–2.

- 2013–14

Maxwell was picked in the Australian A side to play England. He did not bat and went for 0/89 off 27 overs. In the Sheffield Shield, Maxwell made 5 and 6 against Tasmania. He scored 35 and 38 against WA and went for 0/106 off 21 overs with the ball. He did make 4 and 82 against South Australia. Maxwell made 14 and 16 against Queensland. Maxwell ended the summer strongly in a Shield game against NSW. He scored 94 off 95 balls in the first innings, and 127 off 157 balls in the second (rescuing Victoria from 7/32). Against South Australia he took three wickets and scored 119 and 4.

Maxwell was picked in the ODI team against England in 2013–14 season. He took 1-8 and 8, 2-32 and 54 off 39 balls, 0-38, 1-31 and 26, and 22 and 0-25. Australia won the series 4–1.

- 2014: World Twenty20 and other tours

Maxwell was named in Australia's 15 man Squad for 2014 ICC World Twenty20 in Bangladesh. He had a great start to the tournament by making 74 off just 33 balls including 7 fours and 6 sixes against Pakistan in Australia's First group stage match. He finished the series as Australia's second highest run scorer, making 147 at an average of 36.75 with a strike rate of 210.00. Australia again knocked out from the tournament very early.

Maxwell toured Zimbabwe with the Australian one day team for a triangular ODI series. He took 93 off 46 balls against Zimbabwe, 7 against South Africa, 13 and 1–41 against Zimbabwe, 2 and 2–22 against South Africa, and in the final, he caught for 2 and took one wicket for 12 runs against South Africa. South Africa won the tri-series.

Maxwell made a return to the Test team in October 2014 against Pakistan in the UAE, playing the 2nd match of the series. He made 37 in the first innings and just 4 in the second and took 0–78 with the ball. He had better luck in the ODI games, taking 21 and 2-29, 0-19 and 78 off 81 balls earned him man of the match award, and 20 off 21 balls and 2-41 for another man of the match performance.

- 2014–15 season

In the one day games, Maxwell took 29 and 1-32 against South Africa, 0 and 1-20, 1-43 and 2, 1-30 and 7.During the Carlton Mid Triangular Series in Australia in 2014–15, Maxwell scored 1-37 and 0 against England, 0-14 and 20 against India,and 0-22 and 37 against England. In the final against

England he won Man of the Match award for match winning 95 and 4-46.

- 2015 Cricket World Cup

Maxwell was part of Australia's 15 man squad for 2015 ICC Cricket World Cup co-hosted by Australia and New Zealand. He made 66 runs off 40 balls in the first match against England, 1 and 1–7 against New Zealand in losing course, and 88 runs off 39 balls and 1–21 against Afghanistan.

Later on in the tournament, he blasted a 51-ball century against Sri Lanka at the SCG, by recording the fastest century by Australian in ODIs and the second-fastest in World Cup history. It was also during early 2015 that Maxwell broke into the top 10 of the ICC one-day international batting rankings.

He did not bat against Scotland and took 1–24 with the ball. In the quarter final against Pakistan, Maxwell took 2-43 and scored 44 off 29 balls. In the semi final against India, he scored 23 and took 0-18 and helped with a run out. He did not bat in the final against New Zealand, as Australia won the match by 7 wickets and also won their fifth World Cup title. He took 1-37 and ran out a batsman. Maxwell ended the World Cup as third highest run scorer for Australia behind Steve Smith (402) and David Warner (345), scoring 324 runs at an average of 64.80 with a strike rate of 182.02.

- 2015 ODIs in UK

In late 2015, Maxwell travelled to England to play for Yorkshire. He scored 0 and 2 against Somerset, 0 and 23 against Middlesex (but took three wickets), 36 and 140 against Durham, and 43 against Sussex. During Australia tour of England and Ireland, Maxwell played in all ODIs. In one-off ODI against Ireland, he scored only 2 runs and took 2-41.

Against England he made 15 and 1-29, 49 and 2-44, 2-56 and 17, 85 (off 64 balls) and 1-54.He was awarded the Men's T20I Player of the Year at the Allan Border Medal ceremony by the CA in 2015.

- 2015–16 Summer

In the one day series against India, Maxwell made 6 in first ODI, 26 runs in second ODI, 96 off 83 balls in third ODI and awarded Man of the Match. and 41 off 20 balls in fourth ODI. Australia won the series 4–1.

In February Maxwell toured New Zealand with the one day team for 3-match series. The series was not good at all for him. He was bowled for naught in the first ODI, scored only 6 runs in second ODI, and caught for second duck in the series in third ODI.New Zealand won the series 2–1.

In mid 2016, Australia toured West Indies for a Tri-nation series involving West Indies and South Africa. Maxwell made 1-3 and 0 against the West Indies, 2-15 and 3 against South Africa, 46 off 26 against West Indies, and only 4 run in the final against the West Indies. Despite his poor performances throughout the series, Australia won the series by defeating West Indies by 58 runs.

- 2016 and 2016–17

Maxwell was not included for the Test and ODI series against Sri Lanka, but was called to the T20I series. On 6 September 2016, at Pallekele against Sri Lanka, Maxwell scored unbeaten 145 off 65 deliveries which is recorded as the second-highest individual score in Twenty20 International history. Maxwell thus became the first batsman to hit a century in his maiden T20 innings as an opener. In the match, Australia posted 263/3 by recording the highest T20I team total, surpassing the previous highest of 260/6 posted by Sri Lanka against Kenya way back in 2007.

Against Pakistan in 2016–17 season, Maxwell made 60 (off 56 balls) in first ODI, 23 in second ODI, 78 (off 44) in fourth ODI, and 13 in fifth ODI.He was also awarded the Men's ODI Player of the Year at the Allan Border Medal ceremony by the CA in 2016.

- 2017: New Zealand, India and Bangladesh

In January, Australia went to New Zealand for a three-ODI series. In the series, Maxwell scored 20 in first ODI,and caught behind for naught in third ODI. New Zealand won the series 2–0.

In February 2017, Maxwell was picked on the Test match tour of India after New Zealand tour. He played the opening tour game against India A and scored 16 and 1. Mitchell Marsh was picked for the first two tests but then was injured. Maxwell was selected to take his place at number six for the third test.

In the match, Maxwell scored his maiden Test century of 104 off 185 balls and became the second player for Australia to score a century in all three international formats after Shane Watson. His bowling was only used for four overs. He scored 2 in the second innings. Match was ended in a draw. In the fourth test, Maxwell made only 8 and 45 runs, where India won the match by 8 wickets. India won the series 2–1.

In 2017, Maxwell only played one full game in the 2017 ICC Champions Trophy held in England and Walses. In the match against England, he scored 20 runs in a losing course. Against Bangladesh and New Zealand, matches were washed out due to rain by giving one point to each team. Thus, after defeat against England, Australia eliminated from the tournament.

Maxwell was picked on the 2017 tour of Bangladesh. At the press conference, Maxwell said that, "I don't think I will change too much from what I did in India,". "I thought I had really good plans during the Test series against them. I will employ probably something similar, basically backing my defense and trying to revolve my game around that. It is basically going to be batting long periods of time and making sure that when we do bat those long periods of time we are making big hundreds."He scored 23 and 14 in the first test where Australia suffered their first defeat against Bangladesh in Tests.In the second Test, Maxwell scored 38 and 25 not out, where Australia won the match by 7 wickets. Series was shared 1-1. At the end of the tour Darren Lehman said "With No.6 in Australia, it's totally different to Asia. We'll certainly be looking at that position, and anyone can jump out of the pack in the three Shield games and what we think the best make-up is for that first Test. Glenn is there at the moment, like everyone else, he'll have to perform."

Maxwell struggled on the ODI tour of India in September 2017. He made 39 (off 17 balls) in the first ODI, as Australia's top score, then 14 in second ODI, and 5 in third ODI. With poor performance, Maxwell was dropped for the rest of the series and Australia lost the series 4–1.

- 2017–18

In 2017–18 Ashes series, Maxwell lost his spot in the test team for the first test in favour of Shaun Marsh. However he was called up as a possible replacement player when Marsh and David Warner both suffered injury scares the day before the game. He ultimately did not play in the test. During this period in domestic arena, Maxwell scored 278 in the first innings for Victoria against New South Wales. He followed it with 98 against Western Australia. Peter Handscomb under performed in the first two tests and the Australian selectors brought in Mitchell Marsh for the third test, not Maxwell. Marsh played in the last three tests of the series, scoring two centuries. Australia regained the Ashes 4–0.

Maxwell was overlooked for the Australian One Day team in favour of Chris Lynn for the series against England in 2018. When Lynn fell injured the selectors replaced him with Cameron White. The comment by Australian coach Lehmann caused a deal of controversy at the time.

- Captain Steve Smith suggested at a press conference that Maxwell could "train smarter":

He could train a little bit smarter. We've all seen the way he can come out and play and do all his funky stuff and be pretty cool with that. But when he puts his head down he's actually a really good batsman, as we've seen in Shield cricket. If he keeps his head switched on and trains really well and focuses on basic things, probably more than the expansive things, then I think that will help him have his consistency.

- Head selector Trevor Hohns

No-one is in any doubt about Glenn's ability or his potential to produce match-winning contributions with the bat. What we have wanted from him is more consistency but in his past 20 matches in this format he has averaged 22 and we need more than that from a player in the side's batting engine room.

Maxwell later said his parents "were both in tears and pretty upset for me" after Smith's comments. He and Smith subsequently had a talk about what Smith had said. When Aaron Finch fell injured for the fourth ODI, Maxwell was brought into the squad. He played in the game as 12th man, taking a catch to dismiss Chris Woakes. He played in the final game, taking 0-23 and scoring 34. England won the ODI series 4–1.

- Maxwell batting against New Zealand in February 2018 during the Tri-Series

Maxwell was called for the 2017–18 Trans-Tasman Tri-Series involving New Zealand and England. In the first T20I of the tri-series, Maxwell scored 40 off 24 balls which helped Australia to a win against New Zealand.

On 7 February 2018 against England, in the second T20I of tri-series, he scored a blistering 103 runs off just 58 balls to lead Australia to their second consecutive win of the Tri-Series. The innings was not without controversy, as Maxwell was ruled not out on 59 when Jason Roy claimed a catch. With this century, Maxwell joined elite club of players to score more than one century in Twenty20 International history with Brendon McCullum, Chris Gayle, Evin Lewis and record holders Colin Munro and Rohit Sharma. In addition, Maxwell took 3–10 with the ball, including two wickets in consecutive balls. He was Man of the Match for his all-round efforts.

- 2018 South African and England, 2019 India

On 28 March 2018, Maxwell was urgently recalled to the Australian Test squad following the suspensions of Steve Smith, David Warner and Cameron Bancroft for ball tampering during the Third Test of the Australian 2018 Tour of South Africa.He did not play in the third test, however.

In April 2018, he was awarded a national contract by Cricket Australia for the 2018–19 season.

Maxwell was picked on the Australian ODI tour of England. In the first game he was Australia's top scorer with 62. In the three matches he played, Maxwell scored 112 runs at an average of 37.33.He was also awarded the Men's T20I Player of the Year at the Allan Border Medal ceremony by the CA in 2019.Maxwell was omitted from the Australian test squad to tour the UAE in October 2018, which caused some controversy. However he was picked in the T20 squad.

In February 2019, in the first T20 vs India, Maxwell scored 56 and got support from D'Arcy Short who scored 37(37). Australia were set a target of 127. Wickets fell early but Maxwell's innings helped Australia win the match on the last ball. In the second T20 Maxwell scored 113*, thus becoming the first Australian cricketer to score 3 T20 centuries, and third in the world. He got support from D'Arcy Short again who scored 40 while Peter Handscomb also scored 20*. Australia were reeling again in a target 191 as Marcus Stoinis was dismissed early by Siddharth Kaul. But Maxwell's heroics changed the game.He won the Man of the Match award for his blistering century and also won the man of the series for his batting performance of 169 runs in 2 innings.

- 2019 Cricket World Cup and beyond

In April 2019, he was named in Australia's squad for the 2019 Cricket World Cup.

On 16 July 2020, Maxwell was named in a 26-man preliminary squad of players to begin training ahead of a possible tour to England following the COVID-19 pandemic.On 14 August 2020, Cricket Australia confirmed that the fixtures would be taking place, with Maxwell included in the touring party. In the ODI series, Maxwell impressed with the bat, scoring 186 runs at an average of 62, including a brilliant 108 in the last ODI, helping Australia win their first ODI series in England since 2015. He was later named man of the series.

- 2020-21

Maxwell's form continued into the Summer when India toured Australia for 3 ODIs and 3 T20Is. In the first ODI, with the platform of 69 from David Warner and centuries for Aaron Finch and Steve Smith, Maxwell scored 45 off just 19 balls, with 5 fours and 3 sixes but proving expensive with the ball, with figures of 0-55 of 6.4 overs. Despite this, his contribution with the bat was enough to secure a 66 run victory. In the second ODI, again being set a solid platform by the top 4, (Warner 83, Finch 60, Smith 104 and Labuschagne 70) he smashed a brutal unbeaten 63 off 29 balls but once again was poor with the ball, taking figures of 1-34 of 5 overs. Once again though, his batting was much needed as Australia won the match by 51 runs to take an unassailable 2–0 lead over India. In the final ODI, was a shining light amongst a poor Australian performance. Opening the bowling with Josh Hazlewood, he took figures of 0-27 off 5 overs and scored 59 off 38 balls before being bowled by Jasprit Bumrah, as Australia lost the game by 14 runs. Maxwell finished the series with 167 runs at an average of 83.5. In the T20 series, Maxwell was less noticeable, his only score of note being 54 in the final match and only taking one wicket in the series, which Australia lost 2–1. He was not selected for the Test Series.In August 2021, Maxwell was named in Australia's squad for the 2021 ICC Men's T20 World Cup.

- BBL

In the 2012–13 Big Bash League season that summer his best scored of 82 off 50 balls came against the Sydney Sixers.

A Maxwell highlight from 2014 to 2015 season was winning the man of the match in a BBL game scoring 66 against the Melbourne Renegades. In the Shield he took 0/37 against Western Australia, and scored 24 and took two wickets against WA.

Maxwell had a solid 2017–18 Big Bash League season, with scores of 8 (5), 4 (6), 50 (39), 33 (23), 60 (39), 31* (16), 28 (16), 1 (3) and 84 (47) as well as captaining his team the Melbourne Stars to a grand final runners up. That year a report came out which argued that Maxwell was the most effective fielder in the history of the Big Bash.

- IPL

Maxwell first signed for Delhi Daredevils in 2012 as a replacement player for Travis Birt who withdrew from the squad.Maxwell played two games in the 2012 competition. At the 2013 IPL auction, Maxwell was the most expensive player as Mumbai Indians bought him for 1 million US$. In 2014, he was bought by Kings XI Punjab. In his team's opening match against Chennai Super Kings, he scored 95 runs from 43 balls and in the second match against Rajasthan Royals, hit 89 off 45 balls. In the third match, Maxwell scored 95 runs from 43 balls against Sunrisers Hyderabad and was awarded the Player of the Match award for the third time in a row. Later in the season, also against Chennai he scored 90 runs from 38 balls, again winning the Player of the Match award. In 16 games he had the season's third highest aggregate of runs scored with 552 runs at an average of 34.50 runs per innings.

He was retained by Kings XI Punjab for the 2015 IPL Season, but failed to impress with a highest score of 43 and he lost his place in the side, scoring 145 runs in 11 games at an average of 13.18. Maxwell had another disappointing IPL for Kings in 2016 and was bought by Delhi ahead of the 2018 season. He again had a poor season, scoring 142 runs at an average of 14 and not passing 50 once.

In the 2020 IPL auction, Maxwell was the subject of a bidding war between Delhi Capitals and Punjab Kings, before being bought by Kings as the second most expensive buy at IPL auctions 2020.

In 2021, Maxwell was bought by Royal Challengers Bangalore after another bidding war, this time with the Chennai Super Kings. He finished the season as the team's highest scorer, with 513 runs.

CHAPTER TWO

Australia national cricket team

- Australia national cricket team

The Australia men's national cricket team represents Australia in men's international cricket. As the joint oldest team in Test cricket history, playing in the first ever Test match in 1877, the team also plays One-Day International (ODI) and Twenty20 International (T20I) cricket, participating in both the first ODI, against England in the 1970–71 season and the first T20I, against New Zealand in the 2004–05 season, winning both games. The team draws its players from teams playing in the Australian domestic competitions – the Sheffield Shield, the Australian domestic limited-overs cricket tournament and the Big Bash League.

The national team has played 837 Test matches, winning 397, losing 226, drawing 212 and tying 2. As of January 2021, Australia is ranked third in the ICC Test Championship on 113 rating points. Australia is the most successful team in Test cricket history, in terms of overall wins, win-loss ratio and wins percentage.

Test rivalries include The Ashes (with England), The Border-Gavaskar Trophy (with India), the Frank Worrell Trophy (with the West Indies), the Trans-Tasman Trophy (with New Zealand), and with South Africa.

The team has played 958 ODI matches, winning 581, losing 334, tying 9 and with 34 ending in a no-result. As of January 2021, Australia is ranked fourth in the ICC ODI Championship on 111 rating points, though have been ranked first for 141 of 185 months since its introduction in 2002.

Australia is the most successful team in ODI cricket history, winning more than 60 per cent of their matches, with a record seven World Cup final appearances (1975, 1987, 1996, 1999, 2003, 2007 and 2015) and have won the World Cup a record five times: 1987, 1999, 2003, 2007 and 2015. Australia is the first (and only) team to appear in four consecutive World Cup finals (1996, 1999, 2003 and 2007), surpassing the old record of three consecutive World Cup appearances by the West Indies (1975, 1979 and 1983) and the first and only team to win 3 consecutive World Cups (1999, 2003 and 2007). The team was undefeated in 34 consecutive World Cup matches until the 2011 Cricket World Cup where Pakistan beat them by 4 wickets in the Group stage.

It is also the second team to win a World Cup (2015) on home soil, after India (2011). Australia have also won the ICC Champions Trophy twice (2006 and 2009) making them the first and the only team to become back to back winners in the Champions Trophy tournaments. As of 2021, Australia is the only team to win five Cricket World Cups; no other team has won more than two.

The national team has played 153 Twenty20 International matches, winning 79, losing 69, tying 2 and with 3 ending in a no-result. As of November 2021, Australia is ranked sixth in the ICC T20I Championship on 246 rating points. Australia are the reigning ICC Men's T20 World Cup champions, defeating New Zealand in the 2021 final to claim their first T20 World Cup title.

On 12 January 2019, Australia won the first ODI against India at the Sydney Cricket Ground by 34 runs, to record their 1,000[th] win in international cricket.

- Australian cricket from 1876–77 to 1890

The Australian team that toured England in 1878

The Australian cricket team participated in the first Test match at the MCG in 1877, defeating an English team by 45 runs, with Charles Bannerman making the first Test century, a score of 165 retired hurt.Test cricket, which only occurred between Australia and England at the time, was limited by the long distance between the two countries, which would take several months by sea. Despite Australia's much smaller population, the team was very competitive in early games, producing stars such as Jack Blackham, Billy Murdoch, Fred "The Demon" Spofforth, George Bonnor, Percy McDonnell, George Giffen and Charles "The Terror" Turner. Most cricketers at the time were either from New South Wales or Victoria, with the notable exception of George Giffen, the star South Australian all-rounder.

A highlight of Australia's early history was the 1882 Test match against England at The Oval. In this match, Fred Spofforth took 7/44 in the game's fourth innings to save the match by preventing England from making their 85-run target. After this match The Sporting Times, a major newspaper in London at the time, printed a mock obituary in which the death of English cricket was proclaimed and the announcement made that "the body was cremated and the ashes taken to Australia." This was the start of the famous Ashes series in which Australia and England play a series of Test matches to decide the holder of the Ashes. To this day, the contest is one of the fiercest rivalries in sport.

- Golden age

History of Australian cricket from 1890–91 to 1900 and History of Australian cricket from 1900–01 to 1918

The so-called 'Golden Age' of Australian Test cricket occurred around the end of the 19th century and the beginning of the 20th century, with the team under the captaincy of Joe Darling, Monty Noble and Clem Hill winning eight of ten tours. It is considered to have lasted from the 1897–98 English tour of Australia and the 1910–11 South African tour of Australia. Outstanding batsmen such as Joe Darling, Clem Hill, Reggie Duff, Syd Gregory, Warren Bardsley and Victor Trumper, brilliant all-rounders including Monty Noble, George Giffen, Harry Trott and Warwick Armstrong and excellent bowlers including Ernie Jones, Hugh Trumble, Tibby Cotter, Bill Howell, Jack Saunders and Bill Whitty, all helped Australia to become the dominant cricketing nation for most of this period.

Victor Trumper became one of Australia's first sporting heroes, and was widely considered Australia's greatest batsman before Bradman and one of the most popular players. He played a record (at the time) number of Tests at 49 and scored 3163 (another record) runs at a high for the time average of 39.04. His early death in 1915 at the age of 37 from kidney disease caused national mourning. The Wisden Cricketers' Almanack, in its obituary for him, called him Australia's greatest batsman: "Of all the great Australian batsmen Victor Trumper was by general consent the best and most brilliant."

The years leading up to the start of World War I were marred by conflict between the players, led by Clem Hill, Victor Trumper and Frank Laver, the Australian Board of Control for International Cricket, led by Peter McAlister, who was attempting to gain more control of tours from the players. This led to six leading players (the so-called "Big Six") walking out on the 1912 Triangular Tournament in England, with Australia fielding what was generally considered a second-rate side. This was the last series before the war, and no more cricket was played by Australia for eight years, with Tibby Cotter being killed in Palestine during the war.

- Australian cricket from 1918–19 to 1930

Test cricket resumed in the 1920/21 season in Australia with a touring English team, captained by Johnny Douglas losing all five Tests to Australia, captained by the "Big Ship" Warwick Armstrong. Several players from before the war, including Warwick Armstrong, Charlie Macartney, Charles Kelleway, Warren Bardsley and the wicket-keeper Sammy Carter, were instrumental in the team's success, as well as new players Herbie Collins, Jack Ryder, Bert Oldfield, the spinner Arthur Mailey and the so-called "twin destroyers" Jack Gregory and Ted McDonald. The team continued its success on the 1921 tour of England, winning three out of the five Tests in Warwick Armstrong's last series. The side was, on the whole, inconsistent in the latter half of the 1920s, losing its first home Ashes series since the 1911–12 season in 1928–29.

- Australian cricket from 1930–31 to 1945

The 1930 tour of England heralded a new age of success for the Australian team. The team, led by Bill Woodfull – the "Great Un-bowlable" – featured legends of the game including Bill Ponsford, Stan McCabe, Clarrie Grimmett and the young pair of Archie Jackson and Don Bradman. Bradman was the outstanding batsman of the series, scoring a record 974 runs, including one century, two double centuries and one triple century, a massive score of 334 at Leeds which including 309 runs in a day. Jackson died of tuberculosis at the age of 23 three years later, after playing eight Tests. The team was widely considered unstoppable, winning nine of its next ten Tests.

The 1932–33 England tour of Australia is considered one of the most infamous episodes of cricket, due to the England team's use of bodyline, where captain Douglas Jardine instructed his bowlers Bill Voce and Harold Larwood to bowl fast, short-pitched deliveries aimed at the bodies of the Australian batsmen. The tactic, although effective, was widely considered by Australian crowds as vicious and unsporting. Injuries to Bill Woodfull, who was struck over the heart, and Bert Oldfield, who received a fractured skull (although from a non-bodyline ball), exacerbated the situation, almost causing a full-scale riot from the 50 000 fans at the Adelaide Oval for the third Test.

The conflict almost escalated into a diplomatic incident between the two countries, as leading Australian political figures, including the Governor of South Australia, Alexander Hore-Ruthven, protested to their English counterparts. The series ended in a 4–1 win for England but the bodyline tactics used were banned the year after.

The Australian team put the result of this series behind them, winning their next tour of England in 1934. The team was led by Bill Woodfull on his final tour and was notably dominated by Ponsford and Bradman, who twice put on partnerships of over 380 runs, with Bradman once again scoring a triple-century at Leeds. The bowling was dominated by the spin pair of Bill O'Reilly and Clarrie Grimmett, who took 53 wickets between them, with O'Reilly twice taking seven-wicket hauls.

Sir Donald Bradman is widely considered the greatest batsman of all time. He dominated the sport from 1930 until his retirement in 1948, setting new records for the highest score in a Test innings (334 vs England at Headingley in 1930), the most runs (6996), the most centuries (29), the most double centuries and the highest Test and first-class batting averages. His record for the highest Test batting average – 99.94 – has never been beaten. It is almost 40 runs per innings above the next highest average. He would have finished with an average of over 100 runs per innings if he had not been dismissed for a duck in his last Test. He was knighted in 1949 for services to cricket. He is generally considered one of Australia's greatest sporting heroes.

Test cricket was again interrupted by war, with the last Test series in 1938 made notable by Len Hutton scoring a world record 364 for England, with Chuck Fleetwood-Smith conceding 298 runs in England's world record total of 7/903. Ross Gregory, a notable young batsman who played two Tests before the war, was killed in the war.

- Australian cricket from 1945–46 to 1960

The team continued its success after the end of the Second World War, with the first Test (also Australia's first against New Zealand) being played in the 1945–46 season against New Zealand. Australia was by far the most successful team of the 1940s, being undefeated throughout the decade, winning two Ashes series against England and its first Test series against India. The team capitalised on its ageing stars Bradman, Sid Barnes, Bill Brown and Lindsay Hassett while new talent, including Ian Johnson, Don Tallon, Arthur Morris, Neil Harvey, Bill Johnston and the fast bowling pair of Ray Lindwall and Keith Miller, who all made their debut in the latter half of the 1940s, and were to form the basis of the team for a good part of the next decade. The team that Don Bradman led to England in 1948 gained the moniker The Invincibles, after going through the tour without losing a single game.

Of 31 first-class games played during the tour, they won 23 and drew 8, including winning the five-match Test series 4–0, with one draw. The tour was particularly notable for the fourth Test of the series, in which Australia won by seven wickets chasing a target of 404, setting a new record for the highest run chase in Test cricket, with Arthur Morris and Bradman both scoring centuries, as well as for the final Test in the series, Bradman's last, where he finished with a duck in his last innings after needing only four runs to secure a career average of 100.

Australia was less successful in the 1950s, losing three consecutive Ashes series to England, including a horrendous 1956 Tour of England, where the 'spin twins' Laker and Lock destroyed Australia, taking 61 wickets between them, including Laker taking 19 wickets in the game (a first-class record) at Headingley, a game dubbed Laker's Match.

However, the team rebounded to win five consecutive series in the latter half of the 1950s, first under the leadership of Ian Johnson, then Ian Craig and Richie Benaud. The series against the West Indies in the 1960–61 season was notable for the Tied Test in the first game at the Gabba, which was the first in Test cricket. Australia ended up winning the series 2–1 after a hard-fought series that was praised for its excellent standards and sense of fair play. Stand-out players in that series as well as through the early part of the 1960s were Richie Benaud, who took a then-record number of wickets as a leg-spinner and who also captained Australia in 28 Tests, including 24 without defeat; Alan Davidson, who was a notable fast-bowler and also became the first player to take 10 wickets and make 100 runs in the same game in the first Test; Bob Simpson, who also later captained Australia for two different periods of time; Colin McDonald, the first-choice opening batsman for most of the 1950s and early '60s; Norm O'Neill, who made 181 in the Tied Test; Neil Harvey, towards the end of his long career; and Wally Grout, an excellent wicket-keeper who died at the age of 41.

• World Series Cricket and Restructuring

The Centenary Test was played in March 1977 at the MCG to celebrate 100 years since the first Test was played. Australia won the match by 45 runs, an identical result to the first Test match.

In May 1977, Kerry Packer announced he was organising a breakaway competition – World Series Cricket (WSC) – after the Australian Cricket Board (ACB) refused to accept Channel Nine's bid to gain exclusive television rights to Australia's Test matches in 1976. Packer secretly signed leading international cricketers to his competition, including 28 Australians. Almost all of the Australian Test team at the time were signed to WSC – notable exceptions including Gary Cosier, Geoff Dymock, Kim Hughes and Craig Serjeant – and the Australian selectors were forced to pick what was generally considered a third-rate team from players in the Sheffield Shield. Former player Bob Simpson, who had retired 10 years previously after a conflict with the board, was recalled at the age of 41 to captain Australia against India. Jeff Thomson was named deputy in a team that included seven debutants. Australia managed to win the series 3–2, mainly thanks to the batting of Simpson, who scored 539 runs, including two centuries; and the bowling of Wayne Clark, who took 28 wickets.

Australia lost the next series 3–1 against the West Indies, which was fielding a full strength team; and also lost the 1978–79 Ashes series 5–1, the team's worst Ashes result in Australia. Graham Yallop was named as captain for the Ashes, with Kim Hughes taking over for the 1979–80 tour of India. Rodney Hogg took 41 wickets in his debut series, an Australian record. WSC players returned to the team for the 1979–80 season after a settlement between the ACB and Kerry Packer. Greg Chappell was reinstated as captain.

The underarm bowling incident of 1981 occurred when, in an ODI against New Zealand, Greg Chappell instructed his brother Trevor to bowl an underarm delivery to New Zealand batsman Brian McKechnie, with New

Zealand needing a six to tie off the last ball. The aftermath of the incident soured political relations between Australia and New Zealand, with several leading political and cricketing figures calling it "unsportsmanlike" and "not in the spirit of cricket".

Australia continued its success up until the early 1980s, built around the Chappell brothers, Dennis Lillee, Jeff Thomson and Rod Marsh. The 1980s was a period of relative mediocrity after the turmoil caused by the Rebel Tours of South Africa and the subsequent retirement of several key players. The rebel tours were funded by the South African Cricket Board to compete against its national side, which had been banned—along with many other sports, including Olympic athletes—from competing internationally, due to the South African government's racist apartheid policies. Some of Australia's best players were poached: Graham Yallop, Carl Rackemann, Terry Alderman, Rodney Hogg, Kim Hughes, John Dyson, Greg Shipperd, Steve Rixon and Steve Smith amongst others. These players were handed three-year suspensions by the Australian Cricket Board which greatly weakened the player pool for the national sides, as most were either current representative players or on the verge of gaining honours.

- Australian cricket from 1985–86 to 2000

The so-called 'Golden Era' of Australian cricket occurred around the end of the 20th century and the beginning of the 21st century. This was a period in which Australian cricket recovered from the disruption caused by World Series Cricket to create arguably the strongest Test team in history.

Under the captaincy of Allan Border and the new fielding standards put in place by new coach Bob Simpson, the team was restructured and gradually rebuilt their cricketing stocks. Some of the rebel players returned to the national side after serving their suspensions, including Trevor Hohns, Carl Rackemann and Terry Alderman. During these lean years, it was the batsmen Border, David Boon, Dean Jones, the young Steve Waugh and the bowling feats of Alderman, Bruce Reid, Craig McDermott, Merv Hughes and to a lesser extent, Geoff Lawson who kept the Australian side afloat.

With the emergence of players such as Ian Healy, Mark Taylor, Geoff Marsh, Mark Waugh, and Greg Matthews in the late 1980s, Australia was on the way back from the doldrums. Winning the Ashes in 1989, the Australians got a roll on beating Pakistan, Sri Lanka and then followed it up with another Ashes win on home soil in 1991. The Australians went on to the West Indies and had their chances but ended up losing the series. However, they bounced back and beat the Indians in their next Test series. With the retirement of the champion but defensive, Allan Border, a new era of attacking cricket had begun under the leadership of firstly Mark Taylor and then Steve Waugh.

The 1990s and early 21st century were arguably Australia's most successful periods, unbeaten in all Ashes series played bar the famous 2005 series and achieving a hat-trick of World Cups. This success has been attributed to the restructuring of the team and system by Border, successive aggressive captains, and the effectiveness of several key players, most notably Glenn McGrath, Shane Warne, Justin Langer, Matthew Hayden, Steve Waugh, Adam Gilchrist, Michael Hussey and Ricky Ponting.

- Australian cricket from 2000–01

Following the 2006–07 Ashes series which Australia won 5 nil, Australia slipped in the rankings after the retirements of key players. In the 2013/14 Ashes series, Australia again defeated England 5 nil and climbed back to third in the ICC International Test rankings. In February/March 2014, Australia beat South Africa, the number 1 team in the world, 2–1 and overtook them to return to the top of the rankings. In 2015, Australia won the World Cup, losing just one game for the tournament.

As of December 2020, Australia are ranked first in the ICC Test Championship, fourth in the ICC ODI Championship and second in the ICC T20I Championship.

- 2018 Australian ball-tampering scandal

On 25 March 2018, during the third Test match against hosts South Africa; players Cameron Bancroft, Steve Smith, David Warner and the leadership group of the team were implicated in a ball tampering scandal. Smith and Bancroft admitted to conspiring to alter the condition of the ball by rubbing it with a piece of adhesive tape containing abrasive granules picked up from the ground (it was later revealed that sandpaper was used). Smith stated that the purpose was to gain an advantage by unlawfully changing the ball's surface in order to generate reverse swing.

Bancroft had been filmed tampering with the ball and after being informed he had been caught, he was seen to transfer a yellow object from a pocket to the inside front of his trousers to hide the evidence. Steve Smith and David Warner were stood down as captain and vice-captain during the third Test while head coach, Darren Lehmann was suspected to have assisted Cameron Bancroft to tamper the ball.

The ICC imposed a one-match ban and 100%-match-fee fine on Smith, while Bancroft was fined 75 per cent of his match fee and received 3 demerit points. Smith and Warner were both stripped of their captaincy roles by Cricket Australia and sent home from the tour (along with Bancroft). Tim Paine was appointed as captain for the fourth Test. Cricket Australia then suspended Smith and Warner from playing for 12 months and Bancroft for 9 months. Smith and Bancroft could not be considered for leadership roles for 12 months after the suspension, while Warner is banned from leadership of any Cricket Australia team for life.

In the aftermath of these events, Darren Lehmann announced his resignation as head coach at the end of the series with Justin Langer replacing him. On 8 May 2018, Tim Paine was also named as the ODI captain while Aaron Finch was reinstated as T20I captain hours later, although Finch replaced Paine as the ODI captain after the 5-0 ODI series whitewash in England in June 2018.

On 7 October 2018, Australia played their first Test match under new coach Justin Langer and a new leadership group, which included Tim Paine as Australia's 46th Test captain. After a 1–0 loss to Pakistan in a two match Test series against Pakistan in the UAE and a 2–1 defeat against India in a four match Test series, they found success against Sri Lanka, winning the two Test match series 2–0.

In 2019, Australia played in the Cricket World Cup, where they finished second in the group stage before being knocked out by England at Edgbaston in the semi-final. Australia went on to retain the Ashes during the 2019 Ashes series, the first time on English soil since 2001, by winning the fourth Test at Old Trafford.

In 2020–21, Australia hosted India for 3 ODIs, 3 T20Is, and 4 Tests. They won the ODI series 2–1, but lost the T20I series 2–1. Then, the two teams competed for the Border-Gavaskar Trophy which saw one of the greatest overseas Test triumphs by India in the 4th Test to win the series 2–1 with the 3rd Test being drawn.

- Team colours

For Test matches, the team wears Cricket Whites, with an optional sweater or sweater-vest with a green and gold V-neck for use in cold weather. The sponsor's (currently Alinta for home matches and Qantas for away matches) logo is displayed on the right side of the chest while the Cricket Australia emblem is displayed on the left. If the sweater is being worn the Cricket Australia emblem is displayed under the V-neck and the sponsor's logo is again displayed on the right side of the chest. The baggy green, the Australian Test cricket cap, is considered an essential part of the cricketing uniform and as a symbol of the national team, with new players being presented with one upon their selection in the team. The cap and the helmet both prominently display the Australian cricketing coat-of-arms instead of the Cricket Australia emblem. At the end of 2011, ASICS was named the manufacturer of the whites and limited over uniforms from Adidas, with the ASICS logo being displayed on the shirt and pants. Players may choose any manufacturer for their other gear (bat, pads, shoes, gloves, etc.).

In One Day International (ODI) cricket and Twenty20 International cricket, the team wears uniforms usually coloured green and gold, the national colours of Australia. There has been a variety of different styles and layouts used in both forms of the limited-overs game, with coloured clothing (sometimes known as "pyjamas") being introduced for World Series Cricket in the late 1970s. The Alinta or Qantas logo is prominently displayed on the shirts and other gears. The current home ODI kit consists of green as the primary colour and gold as the secondary colour. The away kit is the opposite of the home kit with gold as the primary colour and green as the secondary colour. The home Twenty20 kit consists of black with the natural colours of Australia, green and gold strips. However, since Australia beat New Zealand at the MCG in the 2015 Cricket World Cup wearing the gold uniform, it has also become their primary colour, with the hats used being called 'floppy gold', formerly known as 'baggy gold', a limited-overs equivalent to a baggy green. Until the early 2000s and briefly in early 2020, in ODIs, Australia wore yellow helmets, before using green helmets as in test matches.

Former suppliers were Asics (1999), ISC (2000–2001), Fila (2002–2003) and Adidas (2004–2010) among others. Before Travelex, some of the former sponsors were Coca-Cola (1993–1998), Fly Emirates (1999) and Carlton & United Breweries (2000–2001).

- match records

- Team

1. Australia is the most successful Test team in cricketing history. It has won more than 350 Test matches at a rate of almost 47%. The next best performance is by South Africa at 37%.
2. Australia have been involved in the only two Tied Tests played. The first occurred in December 1960, against the West Indies in Brisbane.The second occurred in September 1986, against India in Madras (Chennai).
3. Australia's largest victory in a Test match came on 24 February 2002. Australia defeated South Africa by an innings and 360 runs in Johannesburg.
4. Australia holds the record for the most consecutive wins with 16. This has been achieved twice; from October 1999 to February 2001 and from December 2005 to January 2008.
5. Australia shares the record for the most consecutive series victories winning 9 series from October 2005 to June 2008. This record is shared with England.
6. Australia's highest total in a Test match innings was recorded in Kingston, Jamaica against the West Indies in June 1955. Australia posted 758/8 in their first innings, with five players scoring a century.
7. Australia's lowest total in a Test match innings was recorded in Birmingham against England in May 1902. Australia were bowled all out for 36.
8. Australia are the only team to have lost a Test match after enforcing the follow-on, having been the losing side in all three such matches
9. The first Test in the 1894–95 Ashes.
10. The third Test of the 1981 Ashes.
11. The second Test in the 2000–01 Border-Gavaskar Trophy series against India.
12. Against India in March 2013, Australia became the first team in Test history to declare in their first innings and then lose by an innings.
13. In the 2013–14 Ashes series, Australia took all 100 wickets on offer in the 5–0 sweep over England.
14. Ricky Ponting and Steve Waugh have played in the most Test matches for Australia, both playing in 168 matches.

- Batting

1. Charles Bannerman faced the first ball in Test cricket, scored the first runs in Test cricket and also scored the first Test century.
2. Charles Bannerman also scored 67.34% of the Australian first innings total in match 1. This record remains to this day as the highest percentage of a completed innings total that has been scored by a single batsman.
3. Ricky Ponting has scored the most runs for Australia in Test cricket with 13,378 runs. Allan Border is second with 11,174 runs in 265 innings a record which was broken by Brian Lara during his innings of 226 against Australia while Steve Waugh has 10,927 in 260 innings.Allan Border was the first Australian batsman to pass 10,000 and the first ever batsman to pass 11,000 Test runs.Ricky Ponting was the first Australian batsman to pass 12,000 and 13,000 Test runs.
4. Matthew Hayden holds the record for the most runs in a single innings by an Australian with 380 in the first Test against Zimbabwe in Perth in October 2003.
5. Donald Bradman holds the record for the highest average by an Australian (or any other) cricketer of 99.94 runs per dismissal. Bradman played 52 Tests, scoring 29 centuries and a further 13 fifties.
6. Ricky Ponting holds the record for the most centuries by an Australian cricketer with 41. Former Australian captain Steve Waugh is in second position with 32 centuries from 260 innings.
7. Allan Border holds the record for the most fifties by an Australian cricketer with 63 in 265 innings.
8. Adam Gilchrist holds the record for the fastest century by an Australian.
9. Glenn McGrath holds the record for the most ducks by an Australian cricketer with 35 in 138 innings.

- Bowling

1. Billy Midwinter picked up the first five-wicket haul in a Test innings in match 1.
2. Fred Spofforth performed Test cricket's first hat-trick by dismissing Vernon Royle, Francis McKinnon and Tom Emmett in successive balls.
3. Fred Spofforth also took the first 10-wicket match haul in Test cricket.

4. Shane Warne holds the record for the most wickets by an Australian cricketer with 708 wickets in 145 Test matches.
5. Arthur Mailey holds the record for the best bowling figures in an innings by an Australian cricketer with 9/121 against England in February 1921.
6. Bob Massie holds the record for the best bowling figures in a match by an Australian cricketer with 16/137 against England in June 1972. That was also his first Test match for Australia.
7. J. J. Ferris holds the record for the best bowling average by an Australian bowler, taking 61 wickets at 12.70 in his career.
8. Clarrie Grimmett holds the record for the most wickets in a Test series with 44 against South Africa in 1935–36.

- Fielding and wicketkeeping

1. Ricky Ponting holds the record for the most catches in a career by an Australian fielder with 196 in 168 matches.
2. Jack Blackham performed the first stumping in Test cricket in match 1.
3. Adam Gilchrist holds the record for the most dismissals in a career by an Australian wicketkeeper with 416 in 96 matches.

- Team

1. Australia's highest total in a One-Day International innings is 434/4, scored off 50 overs against South Africa in Johannesburg on 12 March 2006. This was a world record score before the South Africans later surpassed it in the same match.
2. Australia's lowest total in a One-Day International innings is 70. This score has occurred twice; once against England in 1977 and once against New Zealand in 1986.
3. Australia's largest victory in One-Day International cricket is 275 runs. This occurred against Afghanistan at the 2015 World Cup in Australia.
4. Australia are the only team in the history of the World Cup to win 3 consecutive tournaments; 1999, 2003 and 2007.
5. Australia went undefeated at the World Cup for a record 34 consecutive matches. After being defeated by Pakistan in 1999, Australia would remain unbeaten until they were again defeated by Pakistan in 2011.
6. Australia have won the most World Cups – 5.

CHAPTER THREE

Let's Know About Cricket

- Cricket

Cricket is a bat-and-ball game played between two teams of eleven players on a field at the centre of which is a 22-yard (20-metre) pitch with a wicket at each end, each comprising two bails balanced on three stumps. The game proceeds when a player on the fielding team, called the bowler, "bowls" (propels) the ball from one end of the pitch towards the wicket at the other end. The batting side's players score runs by striking the bowled ball with a bat and running between the wickets, while the bowling side tries to prevent this by keeping the ball within the field and getting it to either wicket, and dismiss each batter (so they are "out"). Means of dismissal include being bowled, when the ball hits the stumps and dislodges the bails, and by the fielding side either catching a hit ball before it touches the ground, or hitting a wicket with the ball before a batter can cross the crease line in front of the wicket to complete a run. When ten batters have been dismissed, the innings ends and the teams swap roles. The game is adjudicated by two umpires, aided by a third umpire and match referee in international matches.

Forms of cricket range from Twenty20, with each team batting for a single innings of 20 overs and the game generally lasting three hours, to Test matches played over five days. Traditionally cricketers play in all-white kit, but in limited overs cricket they wear club or team colours. In addition to the basic kit, some players wear protective gear to prevent injury caused by the ball, which is a hard, solid spheroid made of compressed leather with a slightly raised sewn seam enclosing a cork core layered with tightly wound string.

The earliest reference to cricket is in South East England in the mid-16th century. It spread globally with the expansion of the British Empire, with the first international matches in the second half of the 19th century. The game's governing body is the International Cricket Council (ICC), which has over 100 members, twelve of which are full members who play Test matches. The game's rules, the Laws of Cricket, are maintained by Marylebone Cricket Club (MCC) in London. The sport is followed primarily in South Asia, Australasia, the United Kingdom, southern Africa and the West Indies.Women's cricket, which is organised and played separately, has also achieved international standard. The most successful side playing international cricket is Australia, which has won seven One Day International trophies, including five World Cups, more than any other country and has been the top-rated Test side more than any other country.

- History of cricket to 1725

A medieval "club ball" game involving an underhand bowl towards a batter. Ball catchers are shown positioning themselves to catch a ball. Detail from the Canticles of Holy Mary, 13th century.

Cricket is one of many games in the "club ball" sphere that basically involve hitting a ball with a hand-held implement; others include baseball (which shares many similarities with cricket, both belonging in the more specific bat-and-ball games category), golf, hockey, tennis, squash, badminton and table tennis. In cricket's case, a key difference is the existence of a solid target structure, the wicket (originally, it is thought, a "wicket gate" through which sheep were herded), that the batter must defend. The cricket historian Harry Altham identified three "groups" of "club ball" games: the "hockey group", in which the ball is driven to and fro between two targets (the goals); the "golf group", in which the ball is driven towards an undefended target (the hole); and the "cricket group", in which "the ball is aimed at a mark (the wicket) and driven away from it".

It is generally believed that cricket originated as a children's game in the south-eastern counties of England, sometime during the medieval period.Although there are claims for prior dates, the earliest definite reference to cricket being played comes from evidence given at a court case in Guildford in January 1597 (Old Style), equating to January 1598 in the modern calendar. The case concerned ownership of a certain plot of land and the court heard the testimony of a 59-year-old coroner, John Derrick, who gave witness that.

Being a scholler in the ffree schoole of Guldeford hee and diverse of his fellows did runne and play there at creckett and other plaies.

Given Derrick's age, it was about half a century earlier when he was at school and so it is certain that cricket was being played c. 1550 by boys in Surrey. The view that it was originally a children's game is reinforced by Randle Cotgrave's 1611 English-French dictionary in which he defined the noun "crosse" as "the crooked staff wherewith boys play at cricket" and the verb form "crosser" as "to play at cricket".

One possible source for the sport's name is the Old English word "cryce" (or "cricc") meaning a crutch or staff. In Samuel Johnson's Dictionary, he derived cricket from "cryce, Saxon, a stick". In Old French, the word "criquet" seems to have meant a kind of club or stick. Given the strong medieval trade connections between south-east England and the County of Flanders when the latter belonged to the Duchy of Burgundy, the name may have been derived from the Middle Dutch (in use in Flanders at the time) "krick"(-e), meaning a stick (crook). Another possible source is the Middle Dutch word "krickstoel", meaning a long low stool used for kneeling in church and which resembled the long low wicket with two stumps used in early cricket. According to Heiner Gillmeister, a European language expert of Bonn University, "cricket" derives from the Middle Dutch phrase for hockey, met de (krik ket)sen (i.e., "with the stick chase"). Gillmeister has suggested that not only the name but also the sport itself may be of Flemish origin.

- Growth of amateur and professional cricket in England

Evolution of the cricket bat. The original "hockey stick" (left) evolved into the straight bat from c. 1760 when pitched delivery bowling began.

Although the main object of the game has always been to score the most runs, the early form of cricket differed from the modern game in certain key technical aspects; the North American variant of cricket known as wicket retained many of these aspects. The ball was bowled underarm by the bowler and along the ground towards a batter armed with a bat that in shape resembled a hockey stick; the batter defended a low, two-stump wicket; and runs were called notches because the scorers recorded them by notching tally sticks.

In 1611, the year Cotgrave's dictionary was published, ecclesiastical court records at Sidlesham in Sussex state that two parishioners, Bartholomew Wyatt and Richard Latter, failed to attend church on Easter Sunday because they were playing cricket. They were fined 12d each and ordered to do penance.This is the earliest mention of adult participation in cricket and it was around the same time that the earliest known organised inter-parish or village match was played – at Chevening, Kent. In 1624, a player called Jasper Vinall died after he was accidentally struck on the head during a match between two parish teams in Sussex.

Cricket remained a low-key local pursuit for much of the 17th century. It is known, through numerous references found in the records of ecclesiastical court cases, to have been proscribed at times by the Puritans before and during the Commonwealth. The problem was nearly always the issue of Sunday play as the Puritans considered cricket to be "profane" if played on the Sabbath, especially if large crowds or gambling were involved.

According to the social historian Derek Birley, there was a "great upsurge of sport after the Restoration" in 1660. Gambling on sport became a problem significant enough for Parliament to pass the 1664 Gambling Act, limiting stakes to £100 which was, in any case, a colossal sum exceeding the annual income of 99% of the population. Along with prizefighting, horse racing and blood sports, cricket was perceived to be a gambling sport.Rich patrons made matches for high stakes, forming teams in which they engaged the first professional players.By the end of the century, cricket had developed into a major sport that was spreading throughout England and was already being taken abroad by English mariners and colonisers – the earliest reference to cricket overseas is dated 1676. A 1697 newspaper report survives of "a great cricket match" played in Sussex "for fifty guineas apiece" – this is the earliest known contest that is generally considered a First Class match.

- The patrons, and other players from the social class known as the "gentry", began to classify themselves as "amateurs" to establish a clear distinction from the professionals, who were invariably members of the working class, even to the point of having separate changing and dining facilities. The gentry, including such high-ranking nobles as the Dukes of Richmond, exerted their honour code of noblesse oblige to claim rights of leadership in any sporting contests they took part in, especially as it was necessary for them to play alongside their "social inferiors" if they were to win their bets. In time, a perception took hold that the typical amateur who played in first-class cricket, until 1962 when amateurism was abolished, was someone with a public school education who had then gone to one of Cambridge or Oxford University – society insisted that such people were "officers and gentlemen" whose destiny was to provide leadership. In a purely financial sense, the cricketing amateur would theoretically claim expenses for playing while his professional counterpart played under contract and was paid a wage or match fee; in practice, many amateurs claimed more than actual expenditure and the derisive term "shamateur" was coined to describe the practice.

- The Young Cricketer, 1768

The game underwent major development in the 18th century to become England's national sport.Its success was underwritten by the twin necessities of patronage and betting. Cricket was prominent in London as early as 1707 and, in the middle years of the century, large crowds flocked to matches on the Artillery Ground in Finsbury. The single wicket form of the sport attracted huge crowds and wagers to match, its popularity peaking in the 1748 season. Bowling underwent an evolution around 1760 when bowlers began to pitch the ball instead of rolling or skimming it towards the batter. This caused a revolution in bat design because, to deal with the bouncing ball, it was necessary to introduce the modern straight bat in place of the old "hockey stick" shape.

The Hambledon Club was founded in the 1760s and, for the next twenty years until the formation of Marylebone Cricket Club (MCC) and the opening of Lord's Old Ground in 1787, Hambledon was both the game's greatest club and its focal point. MCC quickly became the sport's premier club and the custodian of the Laws of Cricket. New Laws introduced in the latter part of the 18th century included the three stump wicket and leg before wicket (lbw).

The 19th century saw underarm bowling superseded by first roundarm and then overarm bowling. Both developments were controversial.Organisation of the game at county level led to the creation of the county clubs, starting with Sussex in 1839. In December 1889, the eight leading county clubs formed the official County Championship, which began in 1890.

The most famous player of the 19th century was W. G. Grace, who started his long and influential career in 1865. It was especially during the career of Grace that the distinction between amateurs and professionals became blurred by the existence of players like him who were nominally amateur but, in terms of their financial gain, de facto professional. Grace himself was said to have been paid more money for playing cricket than any professional.

The last two decades before the First World War have been called the "Golden Age of cricket". It is a nostalgic name prompted by the collective sense of loss resulting from the war, but the period did produce some great players and memorable matches, especially as organised competition at county and Test level developed.

• Cricket becomes an international sport

In 1844, the first-ever international match took place between the United States and Canada. In 1859, a team of English players went to North America on the first overseas tour. Meanwhile, the British Empire had been instrumental in spreading the game overseas and by the middle of the 19th century it had become well established in Australia, the Caribbean, India, Pakistan, New Zealand, North America and South Africa.

In 1862, an English team made the first tour of Australia. The first Australian team to travel overseas consisted of Aboriginal stockmen who toured England in 1868. The first One Day International match was played on 5 January 1971 between Australia and England at the Melbourne Cricket Ground.

In 1876–77, an England team took part in what was retrospectively recognised as the first-ever Test match at the Melbourne Cricket Ground against Australia. The rivalry between England and Australia gave birth to The Ashes in 1882, and this has remained Test cricket's most famous contest. Test cricket began to expand in 1888–89 when South Africa played England.

• World cricket in the 20th century

The inter-war years were dominated by Australia's Don Bradman, statistically the greatest Test batter of all time. Test cricket continued to expand during the 20th century with the addition of the West Indies (1928),

New Zealand (1930) and India (1932) before the Second World War and then Pakistan (1952), Sri Lanka (1982), Zimbabwe (1992), Bangladesh (2000), Ireland and Afghanistan (both 2018) in the post-war period. South Africa was banned from international cricket from 1970 to 1992 as part of the apartheid boycott.

- The rise of limited overs cricket

Cricket entered a new era in 1963 when English counties introduced the limited overs variant. As it was sure to produce a result, limited overs cricket was lucrative and the number of matches increased. The first Limited Overs International was played in 1971 and the governing International Cricket Council (ICC), seeing its potential, staged the first limited overs Cricket World Cup in 1975. In the 21st century, a new limited overs form, Twenty20, made an immediate impact. On 22 June 2017, Afghanistan and Ireland became the 11th and 12th ICC full members, enabling them to play Test cricket.

- A typical cricket field.

In cricket, the rules of the game are specified in a code called The Laws of Cricket (hereinafter called "the Laws") which has a global remit. There are 42 Laws (always written with a capital "L"). The earliest known version of the code was drafted in 1744 and, since 1788, it has been owned and maintained by its custodian, the Marylebone Cricket Club (MCC) in London.

- Playing area

Cricket is a bat-and-ball game played on a cricket field between two teams of eleven players each. The field is usually circular or oval in shape and the edge of the playing area is marked by a boundary, which may be a fence, part of the stands, a rope, a painted line or a combination of these; the boundary must if possible be marked along its entire length.

In the approximate centre of the field is a rectangular pitch (see image, below) on which a wooden target called a wicket is sited at each end; the wickets are placed 22 yards (20 m) apart. The pitch is a flat surface 10 feet (3.0 m) wide, with very short grass that tends to be worn away as the game progresses (cricket can also be played on artificial surfaces, notably matting). Each wicket is made of three wooden stumps topped by two bails.

- Cricket pitch and creases

As illustrated above, the pitch is marked at each end with four white painted lines: a bowling crease, a popping crease and two return creases. The three stumps are aligned centrally on the bowling crease, which is eight feet eight inches long. The popping crease is drawn four feet in front of the bowling crease and parallel to it; although it is drawn as a twelve-foot line (six feet either side of the wicket), it is, in fact, unlimited in length. The return creases are drawn at right angles to the popping crease so that they intersect the ends of the bowling crease; each return crease is drawn as an eight-foot line, so that it extends four feet behind the bowling crease, but is also, in fact, unlimited in length.

Before a match begins, the team captains (who are also players) toss a coin to decide which team will bat first and so take the first innings. Innings is the term used for each phase of play in the match.In each innings, one team bats, attempting to score runs, while the other team bowls and fields the ball, attempting to restrict the scoring and dismiss the batters. When the first innings ends, the teams change roles; there can be two to four innings depending upon the type of match. A match with four scheduled innings is played over three to five days; a match with two scheduled innings is usually completed in a single day. During an innings, all eleven members of the fielding team take the field, but usually only two members of the batting team are on the field at any given time. The exception to this is if a batter has any type of illness or injury restricting his or her ability to run, in this case the batter is allowed a runner who can run between the wickets when the batter hits a scoring run or runs,though this does not apply in international cricket. The order of batters is usually announced just before the match, but it can be varied.

The main objective of each team is to score more runs than their opponents but, in some forms of cricket, it is also necessary to dismiss all of the opposition batters in their final innings in order to win the match, which would otherwise be drawn. If the team batting last is all out having scored fewer runs than their opponents, they are said to have "lost by n runs" (where n is the difference between the aggregate number of runs scored by the teams). If the team that bats last scores enough runs to win, it is said to have "won by n wickets", where n is the number of wickets left to fall. For example, a team that passes its opponents' total having lost six wickets (i.e., six of their batters have been dismissed) have won the match "by four wickets".

In a two-innings-a-side match, one team's combined first and second innings total may be less than the other side's first innings total. The team with the greater score is then said to have "won by an innings and n runs", and does not need to bat again: n is the difference between the two teams' aggregate scores. If the team batting last is all out, and both sides have scored the same number of runs, then the match is a tie; this result is quite rare in matches of two innings a side with only 62 happening in first-class matches from the earliest known instance in 1741 until January 2017. In the traditional form of the game, if the time allotted for the match expires before either side can win, then the game is declared a draw.

If the match has only a single innings per side, then a maximum number of overs applies to each innings. Such a match is called a "limited overs" or "one-day" match, and the side scoring more runs wins regardless of the number of wickets lost, so that a draw cannot occur. In some cases, ties are broken by having each team bat for a one-over innings known as a Super Over; subsequent Super Overs may be played if the first Super Over ends in a tie. If this kind of match is temporarily interrupted by bad weather, then a complex mathematical formula, known as the Duckworth–Lewis–Stern method after its developers, is often used to recalculate a new target score. A one-day match can also be declared a "no-result" if fewer than a previously agreed number of overs have been bowled by either team, in circumstances that make normal resumption of play impossible; for example, wet weather.

In all forms of cricket, the umpires can abandon the match if bad light or rain makes it impossible to continue. There have been instances of entire matches, even Test matches scheduled to be played over five days, being lost to bad weather without a ball being bowled: for example, the third Test of the 1970/71 series in Australia.

- Innings

The innings (ending with 's' in both singular and plural form) is the term used for each phase of play during a match. Depending on the type of match being played, each team has either one or two innings. Sometimes all eleven members of the batting side take a turn to bat but, for various reasons, an innings can end before they have all done so. The innings terminates if the batting team is "all out", a term defined by the Laws: "at the fall of a wicket or the retirement of a batter, further balls remain to be bowled but no further batter is available to come in". In this situation, one of the batters has not been dismissed and is termed not out; this is because he has no partners left and there must always be two active batters while the innings is in progress.

• An innings may end early while there are still two not out batters

the batting team's captain may declare the innings closed even though some of his players have not had a turn to bat: this is a tactical decision by the captain, usually because he believes his team have scored sufficient runs and need time to dismiss the opposition in their innings
the set number of overs (i.e., in a limited overs match) have been bowled
the match has ended prematurely due to bad weather or running out of time
in the final innings of the match, the batting side has reached its target and won the game.

• Overs

The Laws state that, throughout an innings, "the ball shall be bowled from each end alternately in overs of 6 balls". The name "over" came about because the umpire calls "Over!" when six balls have been bowled. At this point, another bowler is deployed at the other end, and the fielding side changes ends while the batters do not. A bowler cannot bowl two successive overs, although a bowler can (and usually does) bowl alternate overs, from the same end, for several overs which are termed a "spell". The batters do not change ends at the end of the over, and so the one who was non-striker is now the striker and vice versa. The umpires also change positions so that the one who was at "square leg" now stands behind the wicket at the non-striker's end and vice versa.

• Clothing and equipment

English cricketer W. G. Grace "taking guard" in 1883. His pads and bat are very similar to those used today. The gloves have evolved somewhat. Many modern players use more defensive equipment than were available to Grace, most notably helmets and arm guards.

The wicket-keeper (a specialised fielder behind the batter) and the batters wear protective gear because of the hardness of the ball, which can be delivered at speeds of more than 145 kilometres per hour (90 mph) and presents a major health and safety concern. Protective clothing includes pads (designed to protect the knees and shins), batting gloves or wicket-keeper's gloves for the hands, a safety helmet for the head and a box for male players inside the trousers (to protect the crotch area). Some batters wear additional padding inside their shirts and trousers such as thigh pads, arm pads, rib protectors and shoulder pads. The only fielders allowed to wear protective gear are those in positions very close to the batter (i.e., if they are alongside or in front of him), but they cannot wear gloves or external leg guards.

Subject to certain variations, on-field clothing generally includes a collared shirt with short or long sleeves; long trousers; woolen pullover (if needed); cricket cap (for fielding) or a safety helmet; and spiked shoes or boots to increase traction. The kit is traditionally all white and this remains the case in Test and first-class cricket but, in limited overs cricket, team colours are worn instead.

- Bat and ball

Two types of cricket ball, both of the same size:

i) A used white ball. White balls are mainly used in limited overs cricket, especially in matches played at night, under floodlights (left).

ii) A used red ball. Red balls are used in Test cricket, first-class cricket and some other forms of cricket (right).

The essence of the sport is that a bowler delivers (i.e., bowls) the ball from his or her end of the pitch towards the batter who, armed with a bat, is "on strike" at the other end (see next sub-section: Basic gameplay).

The bat is made of wood, usually Salix alba (white willow), and has the shape of a blade topped by a cylindrical handle. The blade must not be more than 4.25 inches (10.8 cm) wide and the total length of the bat not more than 38 inches (97 cm). There is no standard for the weight, which is usually between 2 lb 7 oz and 3 lb (1.1 and 1.4 kg).

The ball is a hard leather-seamed spheroid, with a circumference of 9 inches (23 cm). The ball has a "seam": six rows of stitches attaching the leather shell of the ball to the string and cork interior. The seam on a new ball is prominent and helps the bowler propel it in a less predictable manner. During matches, the quality of the ball deteriorates to a point where it is no longer usable; during the course of this deterioration, its behaviour in flight will change and can influence the outcome of the match. Players will, therefore, attempt to modify the ball's behaviour by modifying its physical properties. Polishing the ball and wetting it with sweat or saliva is legal, even when the polishing is deliberately done on one side only to increase the ball's swing through the air, but the acts of rubbing other substances into the ball, scratching the surface or picking at the seam are illegal ball tampering.

- Player roles

Basic gameplay: bowler to batter
During normal play, thirteen players and two umpires are on the field. Two of the players are batters and the rest are all eleven members of the fielding team. The other nine players in the batting team are off the field in the pavilion. The image with overlay below shows what is happening when a ball is being bowled and which of the personnel are on or close to the pitch.

- Return crease

In the photo, the two batters (3 & 8; wearing yellow) have taken position at each end of the pitch (6). Three members of the fielding team (4, 10 & 11; wearing dark blue) are in shot. One of the two umpires (1; wearing white hat) is stationed behind the wicket (2) at the bowler's (4) end of the pitch. The bowler (4) is bowling the ball (5) from his end of the pitch to the batter at the other end who is called the "striker". The other batter (3) at the bowling end is called the "non-striker". The wicket-keeper (10), who is a specialist, is positioned behind the striker's wicket (9) and behind him stands one of the fielders in a position called "first slip" (11). While the bowler and the first slip are wearing conventional kit only, the two batters and the wicket-keeper are wearing protective gear including safety helmets, padded gloves and leg guards (pads).

While the umpire (1) in shot stands at the bowler's end of the pitch, his colleague stands in the outfield, usually in or near the fielding position called "square leg", so that he is in line with the popping crease (7) at the striker's end of the pitch. The bowling crease (not numbered) is the one on which the wicket is located between the return creases (12). The bowler (4) intends to hit the wicket (9) with the ball (5) or, at least, to prevent the striker (8) from scoring runs. The striker (8) intends, by using his bat, to defend his wicket and, if possible, to hit the ball away from the pitch in order to score runs.

Some players are skilled in both batting and bowling, or as either or these as well as wicket-keeping, so are termed all-rounders. Bowlers are classified according to their style, generally as fast bowlers, seam bowlers or spinners. Batters are classified according to whether they are right-handed or left-handed.

- Fielding

Of the eleven fielders, three are in shot in the image above. The other eight are elsewhere on the field, their positions determined on a tactical basis by the captain or the bowler. Fielders often change position between deliveries, again as directed by the captain or bowler.

If a fielder is injured or becomes ill during a match, a substitute is allowed to field instead of him, but the substitute cannot bowl or act as a captain, except in the case of concussion substitutes in international cricket. The substitute leaves the field when the injured player is fit to return. The Laws of Cricket were updated in 2017 to allow substitutes to act as wicket-keepers.

- Bowling and dismissal

Glenn McGrath of Australia holds the world record for most wickets in the Cricket World Cup.

Most bowlers are considered specialists in that they are selected for the team because of their skill as a bowler, although some are all-rounders and even specialist batters bowl occasionally. The specialists bowl several times during an innings but may not bowl two overs consecutively. If the captain wants a bowler to "change ends", another bowler must temporarily fill in so that the change is not immediate.

A bowler reaches his delivery stride by means of a "run-up" and an over is deemed to have begun when the bowler starts his run-up for the first delivery of that over, the ball then being "in play".

Fast bowlers, needing momentum, take a lengthy run up while bowlers with a slow delivery take no more than a couple of steps before bowling. The fastest bowlers can deliver the ball at a speed of over 145 kilometres per hour (90 mph) and they sometimes rely on sheer speed to try to defeat the batter, who is forced to react very quickly.

Other fast bowlers rely on a mixture of speed and guile by making the ball seam or swing (i.e. curve) in flight. This type of delivery can deceive a batter into miscuing his shot, for example, so that the ball just touches the edge of the bat and can then be "caught behind" by the wicket-keeper or a slip fielder. At the other end of the bowling scale is the spin bowler who bowls at a relatively slow pace and relies entirely on guile to deceive the batter. A spinner will often "buy his wicket" by "tossing one up" (in a slower, steeper parabolic path) to lure the batter into making a poor shot. The batter has to be very wary of such deliveries as they are often "flighted" or spun so that the ball will not behave quite as he expects and he could be "trapped" into getting himself out. In between the pacemen and the spinners are the medium paced seamers who rely on persistent accuracy to try to contain the rate of scoring and wear down the batter's concentration.

There are nine ways in which a batter can be dismissed: five relatively common and four extremely rare. The common forms of dismissal are bowled, caught, leg before wicket (lbw), run out and stumped. Rare methods are hit wicket,hit the ball twice, obstructing the field and timed out. The Laws state that the fielding team, usually the bowler in practice, must appeal for a dismissal before the umpire can give his decision. If the batter is out, the umpire raises a forefinger and says "Out!"; otherwise, he will shake his head and say "Not out".There is, effectively, a tenth method of dismissal, retired out, which is not an on-field dismissal as such but rather a retrospective one for which no fielder is credited.

- Batting, runs and extras

The directions in which a right-handed batter, facing down the page, intends to send the ball when playing various cricketing shots. The diagram for a left-handed batter is a mirror image of this one.

Batters take turns to bat via a batting order which is decided beforehand by the team captain and presented to the umpires, though the order remains flexible when the captain officially nominates the team. Substitute batters are generally not allowed, except in the case of concussion substitutes in international cricket.

In order to begin batting the batter first adopts a batting stance. Standardly, this involves adopting a slight crouch with the feet pointing across the front of the wicket, looking in the direction of the bowler, and holding the bat so it passes over the feet and so its tip can rest on the ground near to the toes of the back foot.

A skilled batter can use a wide array of "shots" or "strokes" in both defensive and attacking mode. The idea is to hit the ball to the best effect with the flat surface of the bat's blade. If the ball touches the side of the bat it is called an "edge". The batter does not have to play a shot and can allow the ball to go through to the wicketkeeper. Equally, he does not have to attempt a run when he hits the ball with his bat. Batters do not always seek to hit the ball as hard as possible, and a good player can score runs just by making a deft stroke with a turn of the wrists or by simply "blocking" the ball but directing it away from fielders so that he has time to take a run. A wide variety of shots are played, the batter's repertoire including strokes named according to the style of swing and the direction aimed: e.g., "cut", "drive", "hook", "pull".

The batter on strike (i.e. the "striker") must prevent the ball hitting the wicket, and try to score runs by hitting the ball with his bat so that he and his partner have time to run from one end of the pitch to the other before the fielding side can return the ball. To register a run, both runners must touch the ground behind the popping crease with either their bats or their bodies (the batters carry their bats as they run). Each completed run increments the score of both the team and the striker.

- Sachin Tendulkar is the only player to have scored one hundred international centuries

The decision to attempt a run is ideally made by the batter who has the better view of the ball's progress, and this is communicated by calling: usually "yes", "no" or "wait". More than one run can be scored from a single hit: hits worth one to three runs are common, but the size of the field is such that it is usually difficult to run four or more. To compensate for this, hits that reach the boundary of the field are automatically awarded four runs if the ball touches the ground en route to the boundary or six runs if the ball clears the boundary without touching the ground within the boundary. In these cases the batters do not need to run. Hits for five are unusual and generally rely on the help of "overthrows" by a fielder returning the ball. If an odd number of runs is scored by the striker, the two batters have changed ends, and the one who was non-striker is now the striker. Only the striker can score individual runs, but all runs are added to the team's total.

Additional runs can be gained by the batting team as extras (called "sundries" in Australia) due to errors made by the fielding side. This is achieved in four ways: no-ball, a penalty of one extra conceded by the bowler if he breaks the rules; wide, a penalty of one extra conceded by the bowler if he bowls so that the ball is out of the batter's reach bye, an extra awarded if the batter misses the ball and it goes past the wicket-keeper and gives the batters time to run in the conventional way leg bye, as for a bye except that the ball has hit the batter's body, though not his bat. If the bowler has conceded a no-ball or a wide, his team incurs an additional penalty because that ball (i.e., delivery) has to be bowled again and hence the batting side has the opportunity to score more runs from this extra ball.

• Specialist roles

Captain (cricket) and Wicket-keeper

The captain is often the most experienced player in the team, certainly the most tactically astute, and can possess any of the main skillsets as a batter, a bowler or a wicket-keeper. Within the Laws, the captain has certain responsibilities in terms of nominating his players to the umpires before the match and ensuring that his players conduct themselves "within the spirit and traditions of the game as well as within the Laws".

The wicket-keeper (sometimes called simply the "keeper") is a specialist fielder subject to various rules within the Laws about his equipment and demeanour. He is the only member of the fielding side who can effect a stumping and is the only one permitted to wear gloves and external leg guards. Depending on their primary skills, the other ten players in the team tend to be classified as specialist batters or specialist bowlers. Generally, a team will include five or six specialist batters and four or five specialist bowlers, plus the wicket-keeper.

- Umpires and scorers

Umpire (cricket), Scoring (cricket), and Cricket statistics
An umpire signals a decision to the scorers
The game on the field is regulated by the two umpires, one of whom stands behind the wicket at the bowler's end, the other in a position called "square leg" which is about 15–20 metres away from the batter on strike and in line with the popping crease on which he is taking guard. The umpires have several responsibilities including adjudication on whether a ball has been correctly bowled (i.e., not a no-ball or a wide); when a run is scored; whether a batter is out (the fielding side must first appeal to the umpire, usually with the phrase "How's that?" or "Owzat?"); when intervals start and end; and the suitability of the pitch, field and weather for playing the game. The umpires are authorised to interrupt or even abandon a match due to circumstances likely to endanger the players, such as a damp pitch or deterioration of the light.

Off the field in televised matches, there is usually a third umpire who can make decisions on certain incidents with the aid of video evidence. The third umpire is mandatory under the playing conditions for Test and Limited Overs International matches played between two ICC full member countries. These matches also have a match referee whose job is to ensure that play is within the Laws and the spirit of the game.

The match details, including runs and dismissals, are recorded by two official scorers, one representing each team. The scorers are directed by the hand signals of an umpire . For example, the umpire raises a forefinger to signal that the batter is out (has been dismissed); he raises both arms above his head if the batter has hit the ball for six runs. The scorers are required by the Laws to record all runs scored, wickets taken and overs bowled; in practice, they also note significant amounts of additional data relating to the game.

A match's statistics are summarised on a scorecard. Prior to the popularisation of scorecards, most scoring was done by men sitting on vantage points cuttings notches on tally sticks and runs were originally called notches.According to Rowland Bowen, the earliest known scorecard templates were introduced in 1776 by T. Pratt of Sevenoaks and soon came into general use.It is believed that scorecards were printed and sold at Lord's for the first time in 1846.

- thank you for buy & read this book

  have a great day of your
  from : Mr Vivek Kumar Pandey

- This All Credit Goes To My Super Hero Daddy. "Always Love You dad'.

CHAPTER FOUR

Currently Glenn Maxwell Play With RCB

- Royal Challengers Bangalore

The Royal Challengers Bangalore (often abbreviated as RCB) are a franchise cricket team based in Bangalore, Karnataka, that plays in the Indian Premier League (IPL). It was founded in 2008 by United Spirits and named after the company's liquor brand Royal Challenge. Since its inception, the team has played its home matches at the M. Chinnaswamy Stadium.

The Royal Challengers have never won the IPL but finished runners-up on three occasions between 2009 and 2016. Their lack of success over the years despite the presence of various notable players has earned them the tag of "underachievers". The team holds the records of both the highest and the lowest totals in the IPL – 263/5 and 49 respectively.

- Franchise history

In September 2007, the Board of Control for Cricket in India (BCCI) announced the establishment of the Indian Premier League, a Twenty20 competition to be started in 2008. The teams for the competition, representing 8 different cities of India, including Bangalore, were put up on auction in Mumbai on 20 February 2008. The Bangalore franchise was purchased by Vijay Mallya, who paid US$111.6 million for it. This was the second highest bid for a team, next only to Reliance Industries' bid of US$111.9 million for the Mumbai Indians.

The brand value of Royal Challengers Bangalore was estimated to be 595 crore (US$79 million) in 2019, according to a survey conducted by Duff & Phelps.

- Team history

Rahul Dravid was the team's icon player in 2008.

Ahead of the 2008 player auction, the IPL named Rahul Dravid as the icon player for the Bangalore franchise, which meant that Dravid would be paid 15% more than the highest bid player at the auction. The franchise acquired a number of Indian and international players at the auction such as Jacques Kallis, Anil Kumble, Zaheer Khan, Mark Boucher, Dale Steyn and Cameron White. They also signed up Ross Taylor, Misbah-ul-Haq and India under-19 World Cup winning captain Virat Kohli in the second round of auction. The team won only 4 of the 14 matches in the inaugural season, finishing seventh in the eight-team table. Only Dravid managed to score more than 300 runs in the tournament and they had to even bench their costliest foreign player Kallis for a few of the matches due to his poor form.

The string of failures midway through the season led to the sacking of the CEO Charu Sharma, who was replaced with Brijesh Patel. Team owner Vijay Mallya went on to publicly criticize Dravid and Sharma for the players selected by them at the auction and stated that his "biggest mistake was to abstain from the selection of the team."Eventually the chief cricketing officer Martin Crowe resigned.

- At the 2009 player auction, the franchise signed up Kevin Pietersen for a record sum of US$1.55 million, making him the joint costliest player, along with fellow Englishman Andrew Flintoff who was signed up by the Chennai Super Kings for the same amount. They also traded Zaheer Khan for Robin Uthappa with the Mumbai Indians and also roped in local batsman Manish Pandey from them. Ahead of the tournament, which was shifted to South Africa due to the general elections, the Royal Challengers named Pietersen as the team captain for the season. Bangalore continued to struggle during the initial games of the 2009 season, winning only two of their first six games under the new captain. However, the team's fortunes improved after Pietersen left for national duty and Kumble took over the captaincy, as the team went on to win six of their remaining eight league games to finish third on the points table.

The team qualified for the semifinal where they faced the Super Kings.

Electing to field first, Bangalore restricted their opponents to 146 and chased down the total with 5 wickets in hand, thanks to 48 and 44 by Pandey and Dravid respectively. In the final against Deccan Chargers, the Royal Challengers bowlers, led by Kumble's 4 for 16, kept the Chargers down to 143/6. However, they struggled in the runchase, with only four batsmen reaching double figures, and lost the match by six runs in a tense finish.

- Ross Taylor was one of the top performers for RCB in 2009 and 2010

In 2010, the Royal Challengers continued under Kumble's captaincy and finished the regular season with seven wins from 14 matches and 14 points. They were one of the four teams tied on 14 points with two semifinal spots at stake; they qualified for the semifinal as their net run rate was superior to those of the Delhi Daredevils and the Kolkata Knight Riders. In the semifinal, the Royal Challengers were defeated by the table-toppers Mumbai Indians by 35 runs. With a convincing nine-wicket win over defending champions Deccan Chargers in the third-place playoff, the Royal Challengers qualified for the 2010 Champions League Twenty20. Kumble retired at the conclusion of the Champions League, having led the team to the semifinals of both the IPL and the CLT20 that year.

- 2011–2017: Gayle-Kohli-de Villiers era

On 8 January 2011, the IPL Governing Council held the auction for the fourth season of the league. The franchises had the option of retaining a maximum of four players for a sum of US$4.5 million. However, Royal Challengers retained only one of their players, Virat Kohli, leaving the rest of the players back in the auction pool. When other IPL franchises let go the non-performers from each of their teams, RCB lost the top performers from the previous season by releasing them back to the auction pool. On Day-One of the auction, Bangalore bought Sri Lankan Tillakaratne Dilshan for $650,000, their former player and Mumbai Indians spearhead Zaheer Khan for $900,000, ace middle order batsman AB de Villiers for $1.1 million, former New Zealand skipper Daniel Vettori for $550,000, India's new sensation, who played with Mumbai Indians until last season, Saurabh

Tiwary for a whopping $1.6 million, Australia's Dirk Nannes for $650,000 and India's young talent Cheteshwar Pujara for $700,000. West Indian batsman Chris Gayle was brought in as a replacement for the injured Dirk Nannes in the middle of the tournament. Vettori led the side for the fourth season of the IPL.

RCB kicked off their campaign with a comfortable six-wicket win over the newly formed team, Kochi Tuskers Kerala. But then, they suffered three big defeats at the hands of Mumbai Indians, Deccan Chargers and Chennai Super Kings. At this stage, speedster Dirk Nannes was ruled out of the tournament and the RCB team management named West Indian opener Chris Gayle as his replacement. Gayle started off the tournament with a century (102* off 55 balls) against Kolkata Knight Riders, giving the Challengers an emphatic 9-wicket win. RCB also managed to beat Delhi Daredevils and Pune Warriors in their next two matches. They went on to beat Kings XI Punjab by a big margin of 85 runs, after Gayle smashed his second century of the tournament (107 off 49 balls). They won their next two matches against Kochi and Rajasthan Royals, both comprehensively by 9 wickets. They also defeated Kolkata in a rain-affected match at Bangalore. But then, Kings XI Punjab, riding on a blistering hundred by their skipper Adam Gilchrist, ended RCB's 7-match winning streak, with a huge 111-run margin win. In their last league match, the Challengers beat the defending champions Chennai Super Kings by 8 wickets to end at the top of the points table. Chris Gayle, shining once again with the bat, scored an unbeaten 75 off 50 balls.

Royal Challengers faced Chennai Super Kings in the 1st qualifier at Mumbai. Virat Kohli scored an unbeaten 70 off just 44 balls to help RCB put up 175/4 in their 20 overs. Despite losing early wickets, Chennai went on to win the match by 6 wickets. The win took Chennai to the final and RCB faced Mumbai Indians in the 2nd qualifier in Chennai. Batting first, Royal Challengers made a massive 185/4 in 20 overs on a slow Chepauk track. Chris Gayle was the star once again for them as he scored a blistering 89 runs off 47 balls. Mumbai never looked in the hunt for a win as they collapsed to a 43-run defeat. The Royal Challengers qualified for the final with this win and went on to face Chennai at their home ground in the final. Winning the toss, Chennai elected to bat first in the final. The Super Kings posted a huge total of 205/5. The Challengers did not bat well and lost the match by 58 runs. Chris Gayle was named Man of the Tournament and Bangalore set a new IPL record for the most successive wins by winning 7 matches on the trot.

- Royal Challengers Bangalore qualified for the main event of the 2011 Champions League Twenty20 as they finished runners-up in the 2011 Indian Premier League, this made the Challengers the first and only team ever to play in all the three seasons of the tournament. The Challengers, placed in Group B in the first round of the tournament, kicked off their quest for glory with a last-ball defeat to the Warriors. They suffered a big 9-wicket defeat at the hands of the IPL counterparts Kolkata Knight Riders in their second group match, leaving them with two must-win matches in order to qualify for the semi-finals. They registered their first win in the competition, in an emphatic manner, by beating Somerset by 51 runs, thanks to Chris Gayle's 46-ball 86. The win also consolidated their poor net run-rate. In their last group match, they faced the champions from Australia, the Southern Redbacks. Batting first, the Redbacks rode on a century by Daniel Harris (108* from 61 balls) to set RCB a target of 215. The Royal Challengers came out with a spirited batting performance with Tillakaratne Dilshan and Virat Kohli scoring half-centuries. However, the Redbacks hampered the run-chase by picking up wickets at regular stages towards the end of the innings.
- With six runs required off the last ball to win the match, RCB found an unlikely-hero in Arun Karthik, who struck Daniel Christian for a six over deep mid-wicket, to take RCB through to the semi-finals. The Challengers, despite being level on points with Kolkata Knight Riders and Warriors, qualified for the semi-finals on basis of having a better net run-rate than the two teams.

The Royal Challengers played the New South Wales Blues in the semi-finals of the tournament. Winning the toss, Daniel Vettori put the Blues in to bat and the decision seemed to backfire as the Blues amassed 203/2 in 20 overs, mainly due to the efforts of David Warner who struck an unbeaten 123 off just 68 balls. Despite losing Dilshan early in the chase, RCB got off to a rollicking start with Chris Gayle smashing 92 runs from only 41 deliveries. He was ably supported by Kohli, who struck an unbeaten 84 from 49 balls to give RCB a comfortable 6-wicket victory with 9 balls to spare. They took on an injury-hit Mumbai Indians in the final at Chennai. Mumbai winning the toss, chose to bat and put up a modest total of 139 in 20 overs. After getting off to a blistering start with the bat, the Challengers lost wickets at regular intervals before getting bundled out for 108 in 19.2 overs, falling short of the target by 31 runs. Mumbai skipper Harbhajan Singh was awarded the Man of the Match for picking 3/20 in his four overs.

In the pre-season transfer window, Royal Challengers Bangalore transferred Australian all-rounder Andrew McDonald from Delhi Daredevils. RCB paid US$100,000 as transferred fees. Royal Challengers Bangalore also retained Chris Gayle for the next two IPL seasons.

Before the 2012 auction, RCB had got Andrew McDonald transferred from Delhi Daredevils. They had also bought out the contracts of Johan Van der Wath, Jonathan Vandiar and Nuwan Pradeep. In the auction, RCB bought only Vinay Kumar for $1 million and Muttiah Muralitharan for $220,200.

Royal Challengers Bangalore began the 2012 IPL without the services of talisman Chris Gayle who had arrived in India, carrying a groin injury he had sustained in the preceding Bangladesh Premier League. Sreenath Aravind, RCB's most successful bowler in 2011 too was laid low by injury and Harshal Patel emerged as the preferred third seamer in the side ahead of Abhimanyu Mithun. AB de Villiers and Muttiah Muralitharan gave the team a winning start against Delhi but 3 consecutive losses followed. The team rallied back, Chris Gayle finding his touch to hit 5 consecutive sixes off Rahul Sharma and Saurabh Tiwary hitting a six off the last ball to win the team a tight chase against Pune.

- Gayle shone again at Mohali in a comprehensive win while de Villiers, Tillakaratne Dilshan and KP Appanna engineered another win in Jaipur. A washed out match at Bangalore against Chennai denied the team a chance at gaining 2 points outright, the teams sharing points 1-1 each. Two subsequent losses put RCB in competition with Rajasthan Royals, Chennai Super Kings and Kings XI Punjab for the last play-offs slot. Daniel Vettori benched himself so the team could play Muttiah Muralitharan as one of the four foreigners allowed in the playing XI, Virat Kohli taking up the captaincy duties. The team signed Prasanth Parameswaran, who played for Kochi Tuskers Kerala in the 2011 IPL, as a replacement for the injured Sreenath Aravind. A spectacular chase against Deccan Chargers at Bangalore and two routs in Mumbai and Pune put the team back on track for a place in the play-offs. RCB went down to Mumbai in a hard-fought match at Bangalore but bounced back in Delhi as Chris Gayle became the first man to hit 3 centuries in the IPL, hitting

128* at Delhi.

Other results in the tournament now placed RCB in direct competition with Chennai for the final play-offs slot. The teams were tied on points with Chennai ahead on net run-rate but RCB had a game in hand while Chennai had played out their games. A batting failure at Hyderabad in RCB's final game of the season led to the end of the team's 2012 campaign, making it the first time since 2009 that they failed to qualify for both the play-offs and the Champions League Twenty20. Chris Gayle was the highest run scorer of the tournament for the second year in a row, scoring 733 runs at 61.08 with 7 fifties, 1 hundred and a strike rate of 160.74. Vinay Kumar finished as the 5th highest wicket taker of the tournament with his 19 wickets from 17 matches.

Before the 2013 auction, RCB released Mohammad Kaif, Charl Langeveldt, Dirk Nannes, Luke Pomersbach and Rilee Rossouw. At the auction, RCB bought Christopher Barnwell, Daniel Christian, Moisés Henriques, Ravi Rampaul, Pankaj Singh, R. P. Singh and Jaydev Unadkat. RCB kicked off their 2013 campaign by winning their first 6 home games, starting with a 2-run win over Mumbai Indians where Chris Gayle scored 92* off 58 balls and Vinay Kumar picking up 3 wickets. But they suffered a super-over defeat to the newly formed Sunrisers Hyderabad but then they beat the same opponents convincingly by 6 wickets where Virat Kohli smashed a brilliant 93*. They also beat Kolkata Knight Riders by 8 wickets. Gayle and Kohli were in a tremendous form with the bat while Vinay Kumar was the hero with the ball. RCB suffered a shock in the next match against Chennai Super Kings where R. P. Singh conceded a no-ball on the last ball of the match which was a catch. However, the team rallied back to win their next 3 games. One of the matches against Pune Warriors India saw Chris Gayle smash 175 off just 66 balls which was the highest individual score in T20 cricket and RCB put up 263-5 which was the highest total in T20 cricket.

Pune never fought back in the chase and eventually lost the match by 130 runs. People often nicknamed Bangalore as "Ban-gayle-ore". However, the team began to lose matches away from home. One of the matches against Punjab saw David Miller score 101 off just 38 balls to guide Punjab to an unlikely victory. RCB only managed to beat Pune Warriors India and Delhi Daredevils away from home. They were now in direct competition with Sunrisers Hyderabad with 16 points from 13 matches who were also with

16 points from 13 matches. A batting failure against Kolkata and a poor fielding and bowling performance against Punjab at Bangalore left RCB in a do or die situation in their last league match against Chennai Super Kings at Bangalore. Fortunately, RCB registered a stunning win in their last match which was affected by rain. Now, RCB could only qualify for the playoffs if Kolkata would beat Hyderabad. Unfortunately, Sunrisers Hyderabad won the match convincingly by 5 wickets which ended RCB's 2013 campaign. Chris Gayle was the leading run scorer for the team, scoring 708 runs and Vinay Kumar was the leading wicket taker by taking 22 wickets.

Virat Kohli was named the captain of RCB team. Before the 2014 auction, AB de Villiers, Chris Gayle and Virat Kohli were retained from the previous seasons. The players bought in the 2014 auctions were Albie Morkel, Mitchell Starc, Ravi Rampaul, Parthiv Patel, Ashok Dinda, Muttiah Muralitharan, Nic Maddinson, Harshal Patel, Varun Aaron, Vijay Zol and Yuvraj Singh who was the most expensive player fetching a massive 14 crore. They ended up 7th in the points table and didn't qualify for the playoffs in the 2014 IPL.

- RCB retained Virat Kohli, AB de Villiers, Chris Gayle, Mitchell Starc, Ashok Dinda, Varun Aaron, Harshal Patel, Yuzvendra Chahal, Nic Maddinson, Rilee Rossouw, Abu Nechim, Yogesh Takawale, Vijay Zol and Sandeep Warrier for the 2015 Indian Premier League. They also bought Manvinder Bisla and Iqbal Abdulla from Kolkata Knight Riders and Mandeep Singh from Kings XI Punjab during the Transfer Window. They bought Darren Sammy, David Wiese, Adam Milne, Sean Abbott, Subramaniam Badrinath, Jalaj Saxena, Sarfaraz Khan and Dinesh Karthik for 10.5 crore (US$1.4 million) from the 2015 Player Auctions.

Royal Challengers Bangalore started their season with an unconvincing win against KKR at Kolkata, supported by a knock of 96 by Chris Gayle. But they lost their next three matches in Bangalore to SRH, MI, and CSK. Two great bowling performances ensured RCB secured dominant wins against RR and DD, winning by 9 wickets and 10 wickets respectively. Their next match against RR got washed out after a strong batting performance from RCB. They lost a close match to CSK, but recovered by crushing Kings XI Punjab by 138 runs, supported by a century by Chris Gayle, and a four-wicket haul for Sreenath Aravind and Mitchell Starc. Royal Challengers' good form continued when AB de Villiers and Virat Kohli smashed the highest T20 partnership ever (later beaten by the same pair in IPL 2016) against Mumbai Indians, to secure a good win. Later, RCB lost to Kings XI Punjab in a rain affected match, putting their playoff qualification in doubt. They faced SRH in the next match, again affected by rain. Amidst a lot of drama, and stunning performances from Virat Kohli and Gayle, RCB won an unlikely match in Hyderabad. Now, the only way they could be out of the playoffs became very unlikely, yet possible. RCB lost their chance to be placed second in the points table after rain washed out their final match against DD.

They ended the league stage at the third position, with 7 wins from 14 matches. On 20 May, they faced the Rajasthan Royals in the Eliminator and earned a spot in Qualifier 2. However, they lost to the Chennai Super Kings in the Qualifier 2, and ended the season finishing third. AB de Villiers, Virat Kohli and Chris Gayle ended by being the 4th, 5th and 6th highest run scorers of the season respectively, while Yuzvendra Chahal was RCB's highest wicket taker, being the 3rd highest in the season.

- Virat Kohli set the record for most runs (973) in an IPL season in 2016.

In light of financial scandals involving owner/chairman Vijay Mallya, Amrit Thomas became the chairman of the Royal Challengers. RCB changed the team logo and also became the first team in IPL to adopt different jerseys for home and away matches. Virat Kohli, AB de Villiers, Chris Gayle, Mitchell Starc, David Wiese, Adam Milne, Varun Aaron, Mandeep Singh, Harshal Patel, Kedar Jadhav, Sarfaraz Khan, Sreenath Aravind, Yuzvendra Chahal, and Abu Nechim were retained by RCB for the 2016 Indian Premier League. From player auctions, they bought Shane Watson for 9.5 crore (US$1.3 million), Kane Richardson and Stuart Binny for 2 crore each, and Travis Head and Samuel Badree for 50 lakhs each. Other players that joined the team were Sachin Baby, Iqbal Abdulla, Praveen Dubey, Akshay Karnewar, Vikramjeet Malik and Vikas Tokas. KL Rahul and Parvez Rasool also joined RCB for the IPL 2016 edition.

Royal Challengers Bangalore started their season with a blitz from AB de Villiers and Virat Kohli against SRH at Bangalore, to comfortably win their first match. A bludgeoning century from Quinton de Kock meant RCB lost their second match of the season. Their form deteriorated in the coming matches, winning only one match of the next five. Although, Virat Kohli and AB de Villier's brilliant form, along with the emergence of KL Rahul as an important member of RCB's batting, were positive points. Royal Challengers needed to win at least 6 of their next seven matches to have a chance at qualifying for the playoffs. They won matches against KXIP and Rising Pune Supergiant, the new entrant in the tournament. But a loss against Mumbai Indians meant they needed 4 wins in 4 matches to qualify. Since then, Virat Kohli found himself in a sublime form, with captaincy and the bat. RCB most notably defeated the Gujarat Lions by 144 runs, the highest margin in the IPL history.

during this 4 match winning streak. Through other match results, RCB ended at an unlikely second position at the end of the league stage. Virat Kohli dominated the run-scoring list, while Shane Watson and Yuzvendra Chahal collectively topped the wicket taking list at the end of the league stage. They faced the Gujarat Lions in the Qualifier 1 at their home ground, the M. Chinnaswamy Stadium. They won by 4 wickets to make it to their third final in nine seasons. They played the final against SRH, again in Bangalore. RCB lost a hard-fought match by 8 runs, to end as runners up in this ninth season of the IPL. This is the third instance of RCB losing the final in the IPL.

Yuzvendra Chahal and Shane Watson ended second and third respectively on the list for most wickets.

At the launch event of his biography, 'Driven: The Virat Kohli Story' in New Delhi, in October 2016, Kohli announced that RCB would be his permanent IPL franchise that he would play for.

Virat Kohli, AB de Villiers, Chris Gayle, Mitchell Starc, Adam Milne, Mandeep Singh, Harshal Patel, Kedar Jadhav, Sarfaraz Khan, Sreenath Aravind, Yuzvendra Chahal, Shane Watson, Stuart Binny, Travis Head, Samuel Badree, Sachin Baby, Iqbal Abdulla, Praveen Dubey and KL Rahul were retained by RCB for the 2017 Indian Premier League. From the player auctions, they bought Tymal Mills for 12 crore (US$1.6 million), Aniket Chaudhary for 2 crores, Pawan Negi for 1 crore and Billy Stanlake for 30 lakhs. Mitchell Starc dropped out of the season to prepare for the Champions Trophy which led to the management to replace him with Tymal Mills. The team was the worst hit with injuries as their captain Virat Kohli and AB de Villiers did not play for the initial matches which led to the making of Shane Watson as the interim captain. Even their star players KL Rahul and Sarfaraz Khan were ruled out of the season due to their prolonged injuries.

They lost their first match of the season as they were bundled out by 172 and lost by 35 runs to Sunrisers Hyderabad in Hyderabad. But they won their second match against Delhi Daredevils in their home ground. However, they lost the next three matches in a row against Kings XI Punjab, Mumbai Indians and Rising Pune Supergiant respectively. Though AB de Villiers made a quick fire 89 off 46 balls, RCB lost the match against Kings XI Punjab as the other players made 57 dot balls. The match against Mumbai Indians saw Virat Kohli's comeback with a quick 62 off 47 balls and Samuel Badree becoming the 14th player in the IPL history to claim a hat-trick, but they lost the match as Pollard made 70 off 47 balls to win the match for Mumbai Indians. They lost the match against Rising Pune Supergiant by a massive 27 runs. But in their next game against Gujarat Lions, they won by 20 runs and coincidentally Chris Gayle became the first player to score 10,000 runs in T20s.

- However, in their next game against Kolkata Knight Riders, on the day when RCB made 263/5 against Pune Warriors India in 2013 which was the highest IPL score, they were bundled out for 49 all out which is the lowest IPL score and also where no batsman could score 10 runs. They kept losing matches consecutively as they could not make high scores and their big guns – Chris Gayle, Virat Kohli and AB de Villiers failing repeatedly. The pitch in M. Chinnaswamy Stadium was changed from a usual batting to the bowling pitch which made the batsmen struggle for runs. They ended up at the bottom of the table and they changed their squad for each match which was the reason for its downfall. However, they finished their miserable season on a high note after winning against Delhi Daredevils by 10 runs in Delhi. They made low scores like 49 all out against Kolkata Knight Riders, 96/9 against Rising Pune Supergiant and 119 all out against Kings XI Punjab.

- 2018

In the 2018 IPL, RCB ended up 6th in the points table and didn't qualify for the playoffs.

- 2019

Ahead of the 2019 IPL, Royal Challengers Bangalore spent 16.4 crores (US$2.4 million) to buy nine players – Shivam Dube, Shimron Hetmyer, Akshdeep Nath, Prayas Barman, Himmat Singh, Gurkeerat Singh Mann, Heinrich Klaasen, Devdutt Padikkal and Milind Kumar. In-between the tournament, one of the best fast bowlers in the game Dale Steyn joined the squad and was crucial for the team's victories. Unfortunately for RCB, he was ruled out of the tournament after playing 3 matches due to a shoulder injury. Despite their hard efforts, RCB failed yet again to deliver in the group-stages. Out of the 14 games played, they won five, lost eight and tied one. Consequently, they ended at the bottom of the points table for the second time (previously in 2017).

A lot of eyes were laid on the Captain of the team Virat Kohli because he was to lead his country in the upcoming Cricket World Cup, this put a lot of pressure on the captain. In spite of this pressure, Kohli scored a total of 464 runs which included one match winning century and two half centuries, making him the second player to reach the milestone of 5,000 runs in the IPL after Chennai Super Kings' All-rounder Suresh Raina.

Even with RCB's disappointing performance in the season, most of their matches were close encounters and their fans were thoroughly entertained. At the end of the 12th season of the IPL franchise, RCB still remains among the three original teams of the franchise (the other two include Kings XI Punjab and Delhi Capitals) which haven't won the IPL trophy yet.

- 2020

Before the start of 2020 IPL, RCB has released their players: Akshdeep Nath, Colin de Grandhomme, Dale Steyn, Heinrich Klassen, Himmat Singh, Kulwant Khejroliya, Marcus Stoinis, Milind Kumar, Nathan Coulter-Nile, Prayas Ray Barman, Shimron Hetmyer and Tim Southee. During the IPL auction, they added Aaron Finch (4.4 crore), Chris Morris (10 crore), Joshua Philippe (20 lakh), Kane Richardson (4 crore), Pavan Deshpande (20 lakh), Dale Steyn (2 crore), Shahbaz Ahamad (20 lakh) and Isuru Udana (50 lakh).

Vijay Mallya wanted to associate one of his top-selling liquor brands, either McDowell's No.1 or Royal Challenge with the team. The latter was chosen, hence the name.

- Logo

The logo initially consisted the RC emblem in yellow on a circular red base with the black text "Royal Challengers Bangalore" in standard format surrounding the circular logo. The RC crown emblem with the roaring lion placed on the top of the logo was derived from the original Royal Challenge logo. No significant changes took place in the design of the logo except for the replacement of colour yellow with gold from 2009. This logo also had a dotted white circle around the RC emblem. The team also uses an alternate logo for the Game for Green matches where the green plants surround the logo and the text Game for Green is placed below the logo. The logo was redesigned in 2016 with the inclusion of black as a secondary color. The lion emblem in the crest was enlarged and the shield was omitted in the new design. In 2020, a new logo was unveiled featuring a bigger lion and the crown returning from the previous logo. The RC emblem was omitted for this crest.

- Jersey

The jersey colors of the team in 2008 were red and golden yellow, the same as the unofficial Kannada flag, with player names printed in white and numbers printed in black in the rear. Yellow was eliminated in future seasons and was replaced with gold. Starting from 2010, blue was introduced on the apparel as a tertiary colour. The jersey design saw tweaks every season, major being the one for 2014 where blue dominated over gold. From 2014, the player names and numbers were printed in gold. As of 2015, more yellowish shade of gold is being used on the jerseys. The blue was eliminated in 2016 and was replaced by black as the third colour in the two versions of the jersey; one for home matches and the other for away ones. From 2020, black was replaced with a shade between dark blue and black. Reebok manufactured kits for the team from 2008 to 2014 and Adidas supplied the kits in 2015. Zeven manufactures the kits for the team from 2016.

- Theme song

The theme song of the team for the 2008 season was "Jeetenge Hum Shaan Se". The team anthem, "Game for More" was created for the 2009 season. The music was composed by Amit Trivedi and written by Anshu Sharma. A new anthem, "Here We Go The Royal Challengers" was created for the 2013 season and was used till 2015. The anthem "Play Bold" was composed by Salim–Sulaiman, sung by Siddharth Basrur and was released in 2016 during the launch of jerseys for the season. For 2017, the same anthem was recomposed and sung by Anand Bhaskar in 6 languages – English, Kannada, Telugu, Bengali, Marathi and Punjabi.

• Ambassadors

Katrina Kaif was roped in as the brand ambassador for the team in 2008, but later stepped down due to her prior commitments with filmmakers. Deepika Padukone, Ramya, Puneeth Rajkumar, Upendra and Ganesh have been the ambassadors for the team in the initial seasons. Shiva Rajkumar is the brand Ambassador for the season 11.